At Issue

Ethical Pet Ownership: Puppy Mills, Rescue Pets, and Exotic Animal Trade

Other Books in the At Issue Series

At Issue

Ethical Pet Ownership: Puppy Mills, Rescue Pets, and Exotic Animal Trade

Lisa Idzikowski, Book Editor

GREENHAVEN
PUBLISHING

Published in 2019 by Greenhaven Publishing, LLC
353 3rd Avenue, Suite 255, New York, NY 10010

Copyright © 2019 by Greenhaven Publishing, LLC

First Edition

Articles in Greenhaven Publishing anthologies are often edited for length to meet page requirements. In addition, original titles of these works are changed to clearly present the main thesis and to explicitly indicate the author's opinion. Every effort is made to ensure that Greenhaven Publishing accurately reflects the original intent of the authors. Every effort has been made to trace the owners of the copyrighted material.

Cover image: Empirephotostock/Shutterstock.com

Library of Congress Cataloging-in-Publication Data

Names: Idzikowski, Lisa, editor.
Title: Ethical pet ownership : puppy mills, rescue pets, and exotic animal
    trade / [edited by] Lisa Idzikowski.
Description: New York : Greenhaven Publishing, 2019. | Series: At issue |
    Audience: Grade 9 to 12. | Includes bibliographical references and index.
Identifiers: LCCN 2018028210| ISBN 9781534503793 (library bound) | ISBN
    9781534504455 (paperback)
Subjects: LCSH: Pet owners—Juvenile literature. | Pet adoption—Moral and
    ethical aspects—Juvenile literature. | Animal rights—Juvenile literature.
Classification: LCC SF411.4 .E84 2019 | DDC 636.088/7—dc23
LC record available at https://lccn.loc.gov/2018028210

Manufactured in the United States of America

Website: http://greenhavenpublishing.com

Contents

Introduction

"We and our affiliates provide hands-on care and services to more than 100,000 animals each year ... seeking a humane world for people and animals alike. We are ... combating large-scale cruelties such as puppy mills, animal fighting, factory farming, seal slaughter, horse cruelty, captive hunts and the wildlife trade."

—*The Humane Society of the United States*

Dogs, cats, freshwater fish, birds, rodents, reptiles, horses, and saltwater fish—one of these animals probably comes to mind when we think of the pets that people have in their lives. In America, around 85 million people—or about 68 percent of households—report having pets. Dogs are the most common pets and account for almost half of all households. Cats are the next most common companion animal, sharing the homes of roughly 35 percent of the population, while horses and saltwater fish each account for 2 percent.[1]

Owners recognize that pets can impact their lives in positive ways, including providing love, companionship, stress relief, and amusement. Many pet people also admit that they buy Christmas and birthday gifts for their animal friends, and according to the Pew Research Center, roughly 85 percent of dog owners consider their pets to be a part of the family.[2]

With the evident popularity and proven positive benefits associated with pet ownership, one might wonder what possible controversy could be broiling. Not surprisingly, the topic of ethical pet ownership is a complicated one, and debate tends to center around four main topics: the ethics of keeping animals as pets, puppy mills, rescue pets, and the exotic animal trade.

Research and reports by Harvard Medical School detail the ways that dogs improve the lives of their owners and other people.[3] Besides love and companionship, dog owners get more exercise, feel calmer and find it easier to shed stress, and become more social and less isolated as a result of pet ownership. Older individuals reap the same benefits from visits by therapy dogs, and kids can learn responsibility by caring for a pet. Nonetheless, there is the basic question of whether animals should be kept as pets at all. Ethicists argue against keeping pets—which are living, breathing, and feeling sentient beings—for a variety of reasons. They cite statistics showing that many owners never take their dog or cat to the veterinarian, either for wellness checks or when illness strikes. What about wild or exotic animals? Small animals such as reptiles and birds live their lives as pets confined in tiny tanks or cages. Larger species can't possibly be afforded the quality of life they would have in their natural habitats, but this doesn't prevent people from buying tigers, monkeys, and other large wild animals. Buyers fool themselves into thinking that these wild creatures can somehow be happy living in unnatural conditions. PETA, the largest animal rights organization in the world, believes that living creatures should not be under the control of humans in any way: they should not be eaten, experimented on, used for clothing or entertainment, or abused in any form.

The anger directed towards puppy mills is well deserved. "A puppy mill," as defined by the Humane Society of the United States, "is an inhumane commercial dog-breeding facility in which the health of the dogs is disregarded in order to maintain a low overhead and maximize profits." It's hard to believe that the US Department of Agriculture encouraged the dog breeding business that ultimately resulted in puppy mills, but that's exactly what happened after World War II.[4] Soldiers returning from the war faced an agricultural market that wasn't profitable, and something had to replace lost farming wages. At the same time, it was becoming fashionable for individuals and families to purchase purebred dogs as pets. The USDA stepped in and suggested to farmers that they could support their families by breeding purebred dogs. Inexperienced and cash-strapped farmers kept dogs in poor conditions, skimped on food and veterinary care, and focused on profits. Today, "almost all pet store puppies come from puppy mills," according to the Humane Society of the United States, and eager individuals and families looking for companion animals fall prey to this scheme of prioritizing easy money over care for animals. Despite existing efforts to eliminate puppy mills, many more steps must be taken to effectively put an end to them.

Two other options are available when purchasing a dog or puppy. With some research and patience, people seeking a canine companion can avoid supporting the puppy mill trade and instead choose a bona fide dog breeder. Reputable dog breeders aren't in the business to make money off the animals, they only want to recover expenses incurred from raising their puppies. They are often dedicated to specific breeds of dogs and want their cherished puppies to go to the best homes. Consequently, these breeders don't sell their pups to just anyone with cash. They interview potential dog parents, questioning why a canine pet is wanted, and some breeders may insist on visiting a person's home to make sure everything will be right for their pups.

Another option is to adopt a dog, cat, or other animal from a shelter or rescue. Animal shelter or rescue groups can be found in many larger cities, and there are also some organizations operating on the national level. Shelters and rescues get their animals from a variety of sources. Sometimes private individuals can no longer care for a pet and they hand it over to a shelter. Other animals may be rescued from areas hit by natural disasters or from the streets. Some organizations like the Humane Society of the United States employ animal rescue teams that jump in and save animals from puppy mills, animal hoarders, or places destroyed by disasters. And the Society says that "adopting" the 6-8 million animals available yearly "is the best way to find a new pet." However, as the viewpoints in this volume will indicate, there are other ethical and practical considerations to keep in mind regarding rescue or shelter pets. These include whether no-kill shelters encourage shelter staff to adopt out animals that have serious health or behavioral problems and will be excessively difficult to care for, along with whether shelter staff has the right to determine if an animal deserves to live.

Beyond the standard cats and dogs, some decide to own more exotic animals. It is true that some exotic animals look irresistibly cute when young, but those same babies—such as tigers and bears—grow up to become huge, dangerous, instinctually wild creatures that will never become house pets. Keeping reptiles as pets has almost become a fad, but most buyers don't realize the death and destruction that occurs by bringing these animals to market. Large numbers of animals die before they land in pet stores, and wild populations are becoming endangered in their natural ecosystems. The exotic animal trade harms various wild animal populations and can also be harmful to the humans who interact with these species, but despite the myriad issues, it persists. This is because finding ways to effectively monitor, deter, and put an end to the trade is a challenging task, and one that requires coordination among various governments and industries.

Owning and cherishing a pet is a beneficial and rewarding experience for many individuals and families, but it is also a complex matter. As with any controversial topic, committed proponents, opponents, activists, and experts have worthwhile ideas to share, and the viewpoints in *At Issue: Ethical Pet Ownership: Puppy Mills, Rescue Pets, and Exotic Animal Trade* debate and shed light on this important issue.

Notes

1. "The 2017-2018 APPA National pet Owners Survey," by Julie Springer, American Pet Products Association, http://americanpetproducts.org/Uploads/MemServices/GPE2017_NPOS_Seminar.pdf.

2. "Gauging Family Intimacy," the Pew Research Center, March 6, 2006, http://www.pewsocialtrends.org/2006/03/07/gauging-family-intimacy/.

3. "Get Healthy, Get a Dog: The Health Benefits of Canine Companionship," Harvard Medical School, https://www.health.harvard.edu/staying-healthy/get-healthy-get-a-dog.

4. "The History of Puppy Mills and Why You Should Care," by Ivy Collier, Faunalytics, January 1, 2014, https://faunalytics.org/the-history-of-puppy-mills-and-why-you-should-care/.

1

Pets of All Kinds Provide Numerous Benefits for People

FEDIAF

Established in 1970, the European Pet Food Industry Federation (FEDIAF) is an organization representing the pet food industry in twenty-one European countries. It is a partner for European Union institutions dealing with the legislative, political, and technical issues of the pet food industry. FEDIAF supports and encourages responsible pet ownership and recognizes the important role pets play in society.

This viewpoint argues that pets of all kinds provide a wide range of benefits to many people, from pet owners to others who come into contact with these animals. In some instances, pets perform services for people, while other roles include teaching children valuable life lessons, providing companionship, and contributing to therapeutic treatments. To better understand these benefits, FEDIAF supports scientific studies concerning the human-animal bond. This viewpoint presents key findings on the ways interacting with animals can benefit humans.

P ets provide companionship—one of the obvious benefits for their owners. But they also provide far more, as shown by research and scientific studies. As more information becomes available, it can be seen that the human companion animal bond plays a considerable practical and psychological part in today's high-pressure society.

"Overall Benefits," FEDIAF. Reprinted by permission.

For many people, life without a pet would be unthinkable. Pets provide companionship, affection and protection. They can become playmates and partners, with unique bonds being formed between humans and the animals, which become essential parts of their lives. In today's high-pressure society the presence of pets helps many humans cope with increasing stress and anxiety.

The Psychological Role

The pet, in fact, plays a key role in every stage of human development. For the child, a pet animal encourages a sense of responsibility, caring and communication. The relationship instills confidence and friendship—qualities, which can endure and grow as the child moves on through life.

For adults, the pet takes on new roles—providing companionship for those living alone; giving stimulation to make contact with others as in, for instance, an owner walking his dog; and a sense of purpose for the elderly who, with restricted human communication, can give their pet their love and care.

The Health Benefits

For some, the presence of a pet has even more meaning. With training, pets can help their owners to lead a more normal life, as with the case of guide dogs for the blind. Animals are also being trained to help deaf people to identify and react to signals they cannot normally perceive. And, of course, many pets also serve an additional role as protectors or deterrents against intruders.

Assistance animals also fulfill many other invaluable roles, including working as sheep and cattle dogs, as sniffer dogs used for detection of drugs, tracker dogs, mountain, sea and avalanche rescue animals, and police dogs. It is interesting to talk to the handlers of working animals and to learn that they are still regarded as pets, which have simply been trained for specific purposes.

One more unusual use for companion animals is in prisons where pets have been carefully introduced. Staff and inmates alike reap benefits aiding the rehabilitation process.

These qualities and others are increasingly recognised in scientific studies into the relationship between humans and their pets. The coexistence and cohabitation of humans and pets has become an area of investigation in which a growing number of psychologists, scientists, veterinary surgeons and doctors around the world have become interested. In turn, this has led to a wealth of information becoming available.

It has been learned, for example, that the presence of a pet can lead to a reduction in stress, a decrease in blood pressure and the lowering of anxiety levels. Scientific studies have shown that the chances of recovery among pet owning heart patients are higher than among non owners.

Similarly, the benefits for dog owners include improved health through regular exercise. In providing exercise for their dogs, the owners are encouraged into physical activity themselves.

The contribution pets make to society, therefore, goes far beyond the obvious role of companionship. And, in return for the impartial generosity and unbounding affection offered by so many pets, their owners increasingly recognise the need to provide proper care. Above all, perhaps, to ensure their pets receive a properly prepared diet.

History

Companion animals have been part of our lives for most of recorded history and are not just a twentieth century phenomenon. It is not known whether primitive man started first to herd animals for food and campfire scavenging dogs were trained to help, or whether dogs became a part of man's lifestyle even earlier. It is thought likely that the cat's excellence as a rodent catcher in grain stores was exploited by the ancient Egyptians. The question remains, however, did the cat view the human as a superior hunter and simply become domesticated in return for free food?

There are countless historical representations of pets as part of our daily lives. Think of the chivalric knight's tomb with his dog at his feet as a symbol of fidelity, or the magnificent medieval manuscripts with lively dogs, cats and birds tumbling from the margins. Throughout the ages, portraits of royalty have depicted Kings and Queens with their favourite pets.

The ship's cat on Captain Scott's expedition to the South Pole in 1912 was the first of his species to land and overwinter in Antarctica. It had its own blanket, hammock and pillow.

No matter how it first developed, one thing is certain: the powerful bond between people and pet animals is entirely mutually beneficial. Simply to watch a child playing with a pet dog or cat, or an elderly person enjoying the companionship of an animal underlines the mutual benefits and interdependence of the relationship. As is increasingly being recognised, the composite mutual benefits of pet ownership far exceed companionship alone. Indeed, the relationship between humans and animals is far deeper and more rewarding than even pet owners themselves are aware.

Benefits in Therapeutic Context

Pet animals are used for therapeutic reasons in hospitals and nursing homes where the benefits are increasingly being recognised. Patients have something to look forward to and talk about after a pet visit. Although some of these values have been surmised since the eighteenth century, the use of animals in hospital wards is not yet common in Europe. In the United States, more than half of all nursing homes, clinics and hospitals use animals in a therapeutic capacity. Perhaps of all these positive effects on the well-being of a human patient, the most dramatic is that of a dog or a cat in the non-communicative clinically depressed patient whose withdrawal can be gently alleviated by the introduction of the pet. Such practices and their psychological benefits have received endorsement from the medical profession.

Tests have revealed that stroking dogs and cats can lower the blood pressure and heart rate of the human. This may be related to the simple fact that caring for certain pets introduces added responsibilities, such as having to go out to exercise a dog, shopping and generally leading a more active life. Pet owners have often confessed that it is the dog, which makes them exercise. Walking the dog also leads to many conversations and social interactions that might otherwise not have taken place.

Scientific Studies

As part of a wider role, FEDIAF members fully support research into the human companion animal bond. One of the most important international conference on human-animal interactions took place in Prague in September 1998. It was the first of its kind to be held in Central/Eastern Europe.

Some of the scientific research in this area, presented to over 800 delegates at the Eighth International Conference on Human Animal Interactions, included for example:

June McNicholas from University of Warwick, Coventry, UK, who found out that at three months after the bereavement of their partner, pet owners showed fewer physical symptoms, such as crying, than non-owners. Owners often confided in their pets to help release painful feelings at times when sharing these feelings with other people was felt to be socially uncomfortable (*June McNicholas, "Pets as Providers of Social Support: Evidence from a Longitudinal Study of Spousal Bereavement"*).

Dr Karen Allen from the University of New York in Buffalo found that men who own cats or dogs had lower resting heart and blood pressure than non-pet owning males. This indicates that the benefits of pet ownership spread beyond the life shared with the animal, but bring improvements to all aspects of the owner's life (*Karen Allen, "The Healthy Pleasure of Their Company. Roles of Animals in Enhancing Human Health and Quality of Life"*).

2

The Domestication of Animals and Its Impacts

Sylvia Kaiser, Michael B. Hennessy, and
Norbert Sachser

Sylvia Kaiser is an adjunct professor of zoology in the department
of behavioural biology at the University of Muenster. Michael B.
Hennessy is a professor in the psychology department at Wright
State University in Dayton, Ohio. Norbert Sachser is a professor in
the biology department at the University of Muenster.

Domestication has clearly impacted animal behavior in numerous
ways, but this viewpoint also describes how it affects their biology and
development. Evidence provided in the study suggests that a domestic
setting impacts an animal from the very beginning of its life and
continues to affect the animal's development throughout it. Although
there are certain differences found between wild and domesticated
animals of a particular species—including less curiosity but more
playfulness and greater sociality on the part of domestic animals—
certain behaviors are consistent among the species regardless of
whether they are domesticated.

D omestication is an evolutionary process during which
the biobehavioural profile (comprising e.g. social and
emotional behaviour, cognitive abilities, as well as hormonal stress

"Domestication Affects the Structure, Development and Stability of Biobehavioural
Profiles," by Sylvia Kaiser, Michael B. Hennessy and, Norbert Sachser. This article is
published under license to BioMed Central Ltd., August 24, 2015. © Kaiser et al. 2015.
https://frontiersinzoology.biomedcentral.com/articles/10.1186/1742-9994-12-S1-S19.
Licensed Under CC BY 4.0 International.

responses) is substantially reshaped. Using a comparative approach, and focusing mainly on the domestic and wild guinea pig, an established model system for the study of domestication, we review (a) how wild and domestic animals of the same species differ in behaviour, emotion, cognition, and hormonal stress responses, (b) during which phases of life differences in biobehavioural profiles emerge and (c) whether or not animal personalities exist in both the wild and domestic form. Concerning (a), typical changes with domestication include increased courtship, sociopositive and maternal behaviours as well as decreased aggression and attentive behaviour. In addition, domestic animals display more anxiety-like and less risk-taking and exploratory behaviour than the wild form and they show distinctly lower endocrine stress responsiveness. There are no indications, however, that domestic animals have diminished cognitive abilities relative to the wild form. The different biobehavioural profiles of the wild and domestic animals can be regarded as adaptations to the different environmental conditions under which they live, i.e., the natural habitat and artificial man-made housing conditions, respectively. Concerning (b), the comparison of infantile, adolescent and adult wild and domestic guinea pigs shows that the typical biobehavioural profile of the domestic form is already present during early phases of life, that is, during early adolescence and weaning. Thus, differences between the domestic and the wild form can be attributed to genetic alterations resulting from artificial selection, and likely to environmental influences during the pre- and perinatal phase. Interestingly, the frequency of play behaviour does not differ between the domestic and wild form early in life, but is significantly higher in domesticated guinea pigs at later ages. Concerning (c), there is some evidence that personalities occur in both wild and domestic animals. However, there may be differences in which behavioural domains—social and sexual behaviour, emotionality, stress-responsiveness—are consistent over time. These differences are probably due to changing selection pressures during domestication.

Introduction

The development of each advanced civilization was accompanied by the domestication of animals or plants. Hence domestic animals have attended mankind for thousands of years. Most animals living under human control are domesticated. Moreover, domesticated animals play important roles for humans in many aspects of daily life: as pets they are our social companions (e.g. dogs, cats, guinea pigs) and provide protection (e.g. dogs), as farm animals they provide us with food (e.g. meat, milk, eggs) and basic materials (e.g. suet, wax, feather), as laboratory animals they are important for the progress of biomedical research (e.g. mice, rat), and as sporting animals, they even provide us with entertainment (e.g. horses, dogs).

Domestic animals are derived from the wild counterpart by a gradual transformation process over many generations. In most cases wild animals have to adapt to human-made conditions, artificial environments and captivity during domestication. This results in long-term genetic changes and finally in the evolution of the domestic phenotype. Several forces can influence the evolution of domestic animals: sexual inbreeding and genetic drift of small populations in captivity, relaxed selection with regard to certain pressures, such as predation or resource availability, artificial selection for traits preferred by humans like productivity and fecundity as well as for tameness, and finally "natural selection" in captivity for reduced sensitivity to stress caused by crowding, restriction of movement, parasitism and changes in environment and food sources, which finally leads to adaptation.

Thus, the conditions under which breeding, care, and feeding of animals are controlled by humans over a period of generations are fundamental for the process of domestication. This process is always accompanied by distinct changes in morphology, physiology, and behavior. The variability of some characteristics (e.g. body size, colour) is greater in the domestic form. On the other hand, specific domestic characters evolve which are highly convergent between domesticated forms of different species, a phenomenon known as domestication syndrome. Together, these domestication characters enable one to readily distinguish between domestic animals and their ancestors.

In this article we will mainly focus on wild and domestic guinea pigs. Domestic guinea pigs are among the few species that are popular pets all over of the world, used as laboratory animals in scientific research and provide a source of meat, particularly in rural populations of South America. In a first step, we will describe how artificial selection shapes biobehavioural profiles during domestication; that is, how wild and domestic animals differ in their appearance, social and sexual behaviours, cognitive abilities, as well as hormonal stress responses. In a second step, we will discuss behavioural development in wild and domestic animals during the early postnatal phase as well as during adolescence; thus, we will highlight during which phases of life differences in the wild and domestic form occur. In a third step, we will address the question of whether or not animal personalities (sensu) exist in the wild and domestic form, and whether or not changes in dimensions of animal personalities occur during the process of domestication.

[…]

Domestication of the Guinea Pig

The Origin of the Guinea Pig

The guinea pig (*Cavia aperea* f. *porcellus*) was domesticated approximately 3,000-6,000 years ago in the highlands of South America. The Spaniards encountered the guinea pigs in the middle of the 16th century and introduced them into Europe where they rapidly became a popular pet. Nowadays, guinea pigs are one of the most popular pets throughout the world, raised for show and as companions. They also are common laboratory animals in scientific research, used frequently in toxicology, product development and safety testing in the medical field.

The main aim of domestication was to provide the indigenous peoples with meat. Even today guinea pigs are one of the main sources of protein in some rural populations of South America.

Throughout the years, they have also been used in religious ceremonies and traditional healing practices. In South America guinea pigs are left to scavenge in and around the huts of the natives, and it may be assumed that a similar husbandry has always existed.

[...]

The Biobehavioural Profiles of Wild and Domestic Animals in Adulthood

Behavioural Aspects

As indicated above, domestic guinea pigs derived from the wild cavy at least 3,000 years ago. From behavioural observations it appears that the repertoire of behavioural patterns is similar in domesticated and wild guinea pigs, as is the case in other domesticated animals and their wild counterparts. Thus, domestication has not resulted in the loss or addition of behavioural elements.

Distinct differences, however, occur in behavioural frequencies and thresholds: domestic guinea pigs exhibit less aggressive behaviour and more sociopositive behaviour than their wild ancestors. Thus, the process of domestication has led to traits—reduced aggressiveness, increased tolerance of conspecifics—that are typical of other domesticated species (e.g. rats; cats: Zimmermann; mallard ducks: Desforges and Wood-Gush). This shift in biobehavioural profile of guinea pigs likely developed during domestication because of the immense increase in population densities: wild cavies live in large home ranges from 200 m^2 up to 1000 m^2; domestic guinea pigs, however, can be kept in 6 m^2 enclosures with up to 20 adult animals. Housing at such high density is probably possible because early breeders of wild cavies chose and selected for the most agreeable individuals, that is those that were least aggressive toward conspecifics as well as humans.

Other behavioural changes included an increase in the expression of overt courtship behaviour and in the tendency to vocalize in domestic guinea pigs. Furthermore, domestic guinea pigs are less attentive to their physical environment than are wild cavies as indicated by, for instance, the incidence of rearing. This reduction of alertness and sensitivity to environmental change is a further trait typical of domesticated animals. Wild forms of rats, dogs, pigs, and ducks also direct greater attention to the environment than do their domestic counterparts. This is not surprising since a selection against overactive and nervous animals exists during domestication, and sensitivity confers no obvious selective advantage in captivity.

Similarly, domestic guinea pigs show less exploratory behaviour than do wild cavies. A decline in exploration seems to be a general character of domestication that is also found in dogs, rats and mice. In wild animals, exploratory behaviour is crucial for surviving in their natural habitat: animals have to explore to obtain access to vital resources such as food, water, shelter and mates. However, exploring new environments can be very risky and dangerous. For instance, in the natural habitat of the wild cavy *Cavia aperea* predation can be so severe that mortality rates of up to 50% are observed in a five month period. In a second wild cavy species, *Cavia magna*, very high mortality rates also have been shown. In contrast to this situation in the wild, domestication is characterised by a removal of dangerous and challenging environmental factors. In man-made housing systems, guinea pigs are usually provided with all relevant resources and thus the selection pressure for high levels of exploration and risk-taking is removed.

Concerning learning and memory, Lewejohann et al. tested wild and domestic guinea pigs in the Morris Water Maze, a frequently used test for the assessment of spatial learning in rodents (e.g. in guinea pigs). Both wild cavies and domestic guinea pigs were able to learn the task. However, male as well as female domestic guinea pigs showed more-rapid acquisition of the task than did their wild conspecifics. In a discrimination task, domestic guinea pigs also performed better than wild cavies. Furthermore the former learned an association and reversal more-rapidly than did the latter. These findings are comparable to those in rats, in which the domestic form shows equivalent or even better performance in learning and memory tasks than their wild ancestor. Thus, artificial selection and breeding does not necessarily lead to degenerated domestic animals with impaired cognitive abilities.

However, one should always be careful in claiming one form as being superior to the other in learning and memory. Performance can depend on the origin of the animals as well as the type of cues used in the tasks. Domesticated and wild gerbils both born in captivity showed similar performance in an auditory discrimination learning task, whereas gerbils caught in the wild performed more poorly. Wild foxes were less able to learn using human gestures as cues compared with domesticated foxes; however, in a control task using non-social cues, the wild foxes were found to be more skilled. A comparison between dogs and wolves revealed that domestication improved performance in animal-human cooperative interactions, whereas wolves outperformed dogs in an imitation task: wolves learned quickly to open a box after a conspecific had demonstrated how to succeed; in contrast, dogs were not able to solve the task.

Hormonal Aspects

A series of experiments has been conducted to compare the endocrine profile of wild and domestic guinea pigs: while resting, cortisol levels of domestic guinea pigs and cavies in their familiar home enclosure are not different. Wild cavies respond with a larger magnitude increase of their serum cortisol concentrations when exposed to a novel environment than do domestic guinea pigs. Furthermore, serum concentrations of epinephrine and norepinephrine are distinctly higher in the wild than in the domesticated form in response to removal from their homecages. Overall, domestic guinea pigs respond to stressors with a smaller response of the hypothalamo-pituitary-adrenocortical (HPA)— and the sympathetic-adrenomedullary (SAM)—systems than their wild counterparts. In addition, significantly lower cortisol levels in response to adrenocorticotropic hormone (ACTH) application indicate a reduction in adrenocortical sensitivity in domestic guinea pigs. In general, this lower responsiveness can be regarded as a physiological correlate of the reduced alertness, nervousness, and sensitivity of the domesticated animals compared to their wild counterparts. The lower stress response would seem to be sufficient for domestic animals maintained in artificial housing conditions. Wild animals, however, live in much more challenging environments and thus higher endocrine responsiveness to stressors appears to have evolved for this reason. The activation of each of these systems provides the organism with energy and shifts it into a state of heightened reactivity that is a prerequisite for responding to environmental challenges in an appropriate way. Finally, guinea pigs have higher basal plasma testosterone levels than do wild cavies. As mentioned above, guinea pigs also show higher levels of courtship behaviour. There might be a causal relation between higher frequencies of courtship behaviour and higher testosterone concentrations in guinea pigs though the direction of this putative relation is unclear. That is, social interactions including courtship behaviour can result in increased testosterone titers and elevated testosterone can increase courtship behaviour.

Development of the Biobehavioural Profile in the Wild and Domestic Form

In most studies investigating domestication effects, adult animals of the wild and domestic form are compared. Thus, the question arises as to whether differences found in adult animals are already present in earlier phases of life. Here we summarize findings from comparisons of domestic and wild guinea pigs during the early postnatal phase as well as during adolescence, i.e. before and shortly after sexual maturity.

Early Postnatal Phase

Wild and domestic guinea pigs are highly precocial. They are able to feed on solid food and locomote from shortly after birth. Accordingly, maternal care is limited mainly to lactation and grooming. Remarkably, domestic females suckle their male and female offspring significantly longer than do wild females in comparable environments with the same diet available, suggesting increased maternal care in the domestic form.

Sabaß recorded the behaviour of male and female wild and domestic guinea pigs on day 11, 15 and 19 after birth, that is, up to shortly before weaning which occurs at about 21 days of age. Aggressive as well as courtship and sexual behaviour were only rarely shown by infant animals, and no differences in these behaviours could be found between the two different forms. Significant differences occurred, however, for sociopositive behaviour and attentiveness: Infant male and female domestic guinea pigs showed longer duration of *bodily contact* with their parents than did infant wild cavies at all three observation days, and infants of the domestic form were less attentive to their environment than same-aged wild cavies. Thus, these findings during the early postnatal phase of life replicate the differences described in adult animals. Interestingly, comparable amounts of play behaviour were shown by infant wild and domestic animals. In this species play is primarily solitary and consists of *frisky hops* (executing upward leaps and turning the head or foreparts sharply while in the air) and *run off* (starting with a short and fast run, then stopping suddenly and changing direction). Generally, it is assumed that play is important for developmental processes by, for example, stimulating muscle growth. If there are similar requirements for these developmental processes for pups of both the domestic and wild form, there might be a similar selection pressure on young wild and domestic animals to play during early phases of life. In adulthood, however, male guinea pigs play more often than male wild cavies. Other domesticated animals, such as dogs and cats exhibit apparent play in adulthood, whereas their wild ancestors play only at younger ages, Sambraus 1978 and Stauffacher 1990 cited in. During the process of domestication, animals typically live under conditions in which predators are rare or absent and important resources are sufficiently available;

that is, domesticated animals mainly exist in relaxed, non-stressed situations over generations. Generally, play occurs only in such situations. Thus, the threshold for play behaviour in domesticated adults might be reduced. Another explanation is that domestication results in retarded behavioural development, or in the retention of juvenile features into sexual maturity, a phenomenon known as neoteny. It may be that the more frequent display of play behaviour in adult domestic guinea pigs in comparison to the wild form is a sign of neoteny.

Adolescence

In a recent study, we have compared the biobehavioural profile in domestic guinea pigs and wild cavies from early to late adolescence. Three different domains of the biobehavioural profile were investigated: anxiety-like and risk-taking behaviour, social and courtship behaviour as well as cortisol stress responses. To assess anxiety-like behaviour, the animal was placed into an open arena (open-field test), and the percentage of time that the individual spent away from the walls in the central area was recorded. As a further measure of anxiety-like behaviour, the latency to leave a dark box, and the percentage of time spent in a light area, were recorded in the dark-light-test. Risk-taking behaviour was measured in the step-down-test, in which the animal is placed on an elevated platform and the latency to step down is recorded. Social and courtship behaviour were assessed in two tests in which the animals were either introduced to an unfamiliar infant or an unfamiliar non-oestrous female. In these tests the latencies to approach the unfamiliar individuals and the frequencies of contact and courtship behaviour, respectively, were recorded. Finally, stress reactivity was assessed by placing the animals singly into an unfamiliar enclosure and by determining serum cortisol concentrations at the beginning of each test (basal values) as well as 1, 2 and 4 hours later. All tests were conducted twice: during early adolescence (at about 50 to 60 days of age) that is, before reaching sexual maturity—which occurs around

75 days of age—as well as during late adolescence (at about 120 to 130 days of age).

Early and late adolescent domestic guinea pigs showed more anxiety-like behaviour in the open-field and dark-light test in comparison to the wild form. Furthermore, domesticated animals were less likely to take risks in the form of descending from the elevated platform. Regarding social behaviour, early and late adolescent male guinea pigs directed more social activity towards unfamiliar females and infants than did same-aged male wild cavies. Finally, the cortisol response to a novel environment was significantly higher in early and late adolescent wild cavies compared to early and late adolescent domestic guinea pigs. In contrast, basal values of cortisol reflecting conditions in the familiar home enclosure did not differ between the wild and domestic form. Basal testosterone concentrations were markedly higher in guinea pigs than wild cavies in early as well as late adolescence. As referred to earlier, the latter result may be related to the increased levels of courtship and sexual behaviour, which frequently are found in domesticated animals. In summary, the comparison of wild cavies and domestic guinea pigs from early to late adolescence replicate the results obtained in earlier studies of adult animals.

Effects of Domestication on Animal Personality

Biobehavioural profiles may vary conspicuously between members of the same species. Understanding such variation is of major importance because it is frequently related to differences in reproductive success, susceptibility to disease and quality of life. If an individual biobehavioural profile is consistent over time and/ or across contexts, it is often described as "animal personality." An ever increasing number of reports show that animal personalities are widespread across a great variety of taxa, including fish, birds and mammals, and even invertebrates.

It would be of interest to know whether or not the same behavioural and physiological traits are stable over time and/ or across context in the domestic form as compared to the wild ancestor. To our knowledge, there are no studies in this area that directly compare the domestic and wild forms. However, Zipser et al. recently published a study regarding animal personalities in domestic guinea pigs and Guenther and Trillmich provided data for the wild cavy.

In domestic guinea pigs, Zipser et al. investigated the temporal stability of personality traits in adult males, namely courtship and sexual behaviour displayed with an unfamiliar, non-oestrous female, risk-taking as well as anxiety-like behaviour in novel environments and cortisol-stress reactivity in a challenging situation. The males were 7 to 18 months old and were tested twice at an interval of 2 months. Sexual and courtship behaviour displayed a clear consistency over time. The more sexual and courtship behaviour a male exhibited during the first test, the more he showed during the second. This agrees with findings in pioneering work on guinea pigs by Young and colleagues, in which males were exposed to an unfamiliar oestrus female and a sex drive score was calculated from the courtship and sexual behaviour displayed. When tested repeatedly over time, highly stable sex drive scores were found. After castration, sexual behaviour declined strongly in all males, but was restored by experimental androgen replacement. Remarkably, after androgen replacement therapy the males' sex drive scores returned to their individual pre-castration levels, irrespective of the dosage of androgen.

Stress reactivity in domestic guinea pigs exposed to a novel enclosure showed substantial individual variation. As was the case for social behaviour, this individual stress reactivity was very stable over time. The higher the cortisol response during the first challenge test, the higher the response when tested for the second time about 2 months later. It appears that such clear individual stability of cortisol responsiveness over time has only rarely been shown in an animal model.

In contrast to social behaviour and acute stress responsiveness, no consistency was found for emotional behaviour: Neither anxiety-like nor risk-taking behaviour proved to be stable over time. It is somewhat surprising then that in the Guenther and Trillmich study investigating anxiety-like and risk-taking behaviour in wild cavies the opposite conclusion was drawn. In that study an open-field-test, a long-field and a novel-object test were conducted. In the long-field test, a 5-m long corridor was attached to the standard housing enclosure so that the animals could freely explore the new environment. In the novel object test, an unfamiliar object such as a red plastic toy pig was introduced into the homecage. Parameters such as distance traversed in the open-field-test, latency to initiate exploration in the long-field test and to contact the novel object were used to estimate anxiety-like reactions and risk-taking. In contrast to domestic guinea pigs, individual emotional behaviour in terms of latency to explore in the long-field-test as well as of distance explored in the open-field-test was stable over time in the wild ancestor.

How might this difference between the wild and domestic form be reconciled? Current theories on the emergence of personality traits emphasize the importance of unpredictable environments. In especially uncertain or ever-changing environments, one strategy would be for individuals to continually change their behavioural responses to adjust to the environmental changes. This strategy is not only very costly it also involves the risk that appropriate behavioural adjustment will repeatedly lag behind environmental change. In such situations, it may be a better strategy to develop stable traits of behavioural responses which may be inappropriate in some situations, but are effective in most. This line of reasoning may help to account for the differences in personalities of wild cavies and domestic guinea pigs. In the natural habitat of wild cavies, the environment is rather unpredictable due to heavy predation pressure and tremendous fluctuations of population densities. In this situation stable emotional traits seem to be adaptive. Because these environmental influences are removed during domestication, stable emotional responses are no longer necessary, and thus may be lost in domestic guinea pigs.

Conclusion

Domestication is a complex evolutionary process bringing about significant changes in biobehavioural profiles. There is growing evidence that the differences in behavioural and endocrine traits between domestic and wild animals of the same species reflect the different demands of the natural habitat in which wild animals are living and of the man-made artificial conditions to which domestic animals are exposed. Compared to domestic animals, the wild ancestor is generally characterized by greater exploration and risk-taking as well as less anxiety-like behaviour. These behavioural patterns presumably help the animals to cope with the ever changing and fluctuating conditions of the natural habitat. Furthermore, animals of the wild form are characterized by more-vigorous stress responsiveness. Since the increase of glucocorticoids and catecholamines ultimately provides the animal with more energy, it seems likely that robust responsiveness of the stress hormone systems is a prerequisite for coping successfully with the demands of the ecological niche, e.g., high predation pressure. In contrast, domestic guinea pigs are more sociable and less aggressive. These traits facilitate survival in the dense housing conditions in which domestic animals often are maintained. Domestic guinea pigs also explore less and take fewer risks, probably because in man-made housing conditions all relevant resources such as food are available. Finally, the domestic form shows diminished stress responsiveness. This trait may be regarded as an adaptation since the less-challenging housing conditions do not require excessive energy expenditure and thus robust stress responsiveness may be wasteful rather than valuable. A further domestication character is reduction in brain weight. In guinea pigs for example brain weight is reduced by about 13% in comparison to wild cavies. For many years, it was assumed that this trait was accompanied by reduced cognitive abilities. Recent studies comparing wild and domestic animals, however, suggest that domestic animals are not inferior with respect to memory and learning.

In most studies investigating domestication effects, adult animals of the domestic and wild form are compared. Here we show that differences between the biobehavioural profiles of guinea pigs and their wild ancestor are already present during early stages of life, i.e. during the early postnatal phase as well as early and late adolescence. While differences between the domestic and wild form almost certainly involve genetic alterations brought about by artificial selection during the process of domestication, they may also be due to environmental conditions and social experiences during the prenatal and perinatal phase that differentially influence brain development in domestic and wild forms. Such early influences leading to different biobehavioural profiles were shown to be mediated by epigenetic effects, which can be stable over generations.

Finally, we provide evidence that personalities occur in both wild and domestic animals. However, there appear to be differences in which behavioural domains are stable over time. In domestic guinea pigs, social and sexual behaviour as well as cortisol stress-reactivity show good temporal stability, whereas emotional behaviour does not. This contrasts with the wild ancestor in which emotional behaviour does appear stable over time. These initial findings on the effect of domestication on animal personality are intriguing, though much remains to be learned. This is, perhaps, one of the most fertile areas for future research on the domestication process.

3

Pets Aren't That Happy—Is It Selfish or Wrong to Keep Animals as Pets?

Melissa Dahl

Melissa Dahl is a journalist and senior editor at New York Magazine's the Cut.

Is it selfish or even wrong to have pets? Some bioethicists are giving this question serious consideration. While many pet owners profess to love their animals, recent studies suggest that pets are not always well cared for—some animals don't get enough exercise, attention, or veterinary care, and they might be bored or lonely. The viewpoint considers this question through discussing findings from the book Run, Spot, Run, *which was written by the bioethicist Jessica Pierce.*

It's the seemingly lightweight question at the heart of *The Secret Life of Pets*—or, at least, at the heart of its ad campaign: What do pets do all day? The film spends most of its running time detailing an unusually adventurous day for this particular band of New York City companion animals, but it also gives the viewers a hint about what they get up to in a typical day; for some of them, it's not much, actually. One character in particular—the canine protagonist, Max, voiced by Louis C.K.—spends most of his day staring longingly at the door of the small apartment he shares with his beloved owner, Katie, as he waits for her to come home.

"Are Pets As Happy As Their Owners Think They Are?" by Melissa Dahl, New York Media LLC, July 20, 2016. Reprinted by permission.

But there's another question that film only sort of asks, and then only sort of answers. As much as people love their pets, how selfish is the pet-human relationship, really? It's something a few critics have already picked up on. "There are intriguing tensions in the subtext that the movie does its absolute best not to explore. (Is it better to be a free pet or a pet in fealty to humans? Does human love make up for being trapped in a 600 square-foot apartment for 22 hours a day?)" *The Atlantic* noted in its review.

If the ethics of pet-keeping provides the barest of subtext for *The Secret Life of Pets* (and, as such, had me feeling vaguely uncomfortable as I left the theater), a recent book tackles the issue with an excruciatingly straightforward manner. In writing *Run, Spot, Run*, published by the University of Chicago Press in May, bioethicist Jessica Pierce has clearly thought deeply about the "ambiguous ethics" of the practice of pet ownership. It's a more complicated commitment than it's often seen as, she writes; as a consequence, sometimes even our best intentions backfire. (Reminder: Dogs hate hugs.)

In the US, there are about 470 million pets and about 316 million people, according to Pierce, and too many of them aren't well cared for. (A quick note: Pierce's book covers all sorts of animals, from cats and dogs to birds, reptiles, rodents, and even exotic animals; for simplicity's sake, I'll be focusing here on cats and dogs.) "Pet owners, on average, spend far less than they should on veterinary care," she writes. "At least a quarter of all dogs and cats never see a veterinarian, and millions live with untreated chronic pain or slow-moving illnesses that owners either fail to notice or are too tightfisted to address." On the other hand, there are those of us who spend exorbitant amounts of money on veterinary care; we're not exempt, either, Pierce argues. Our furry friends bring us so much joy and meaning to our lives, but is the feeling necessarily mutual? And, perhaps more important: How many pet owners have even stopped to consider the question?

It seems, at first, like a fairly ridiculous question. Pets have it easy! They don't have to hunt for their food; you buy it for them and serve it to them. They don't have to worry about predators; you provide them with shelter and a place to sleep (and, chances are, that place is your own bed). You provide them with medical care, you take them out for exercise—you literally *clean up their sh*t*, for heaven's sake. What more could they need? "All of these things are pretty clearly good for our animals," Pierce said in an interview with *Science of Us*. "But the downside is that they don't really have anything to *do* ... We make them really dependent on us, by socializing them to be indoor animals. And then we leave! We leave them at home alone, which is hard on a lot of animals."

There is a faintly unbelievable statistic Pierce cites in her book, taken from the American Time Use Survey: pet owners spend, on average, just 40 minutes per day on "pet care"—that is, feeding, grooming, exercising, and playing with their animals. It's worth being skeptical of that figure; it's just an average, and it's often hard to tell much from averages. Some people surely spend much more time with their pets, while others spend less. Pierce agreed the number did seem unusually low to her, too, but thinks it might be like the TV-watching statistics, which seem incredibly high, until you think through your own time spent watching television.

At any rate, even the most-loved pets are often bored and lonely, she writes in her book; in a way, it's the same paradox many zoos are facing with their animals. "You hear this all the time," she said. "They say, 'Well, these animals are really well off, because they don't have to get their own food—we give it to them—and they don't have to protect themselves from predators—we do that for them. The problem is they are behaviorally evolved to do those jobs themselves. So it's leaving all these behavioral needs unmet." Some zoos now are beginning to address this problem by looking for enrichment opportunities, defined recently by one team of scientists as "making changes to an animal's environment that provide the animal with added stimulation, choice or control." There is, alas, little academic research concerning enrichment as it applies to domesticated animals—most of it focuses on zoo animals—but animal behavior experts have some ideas of how to make your pets' lives happier.

Let's start with cats, who, it turns out, are not exactly the easy pets their reputation would have you believe, said Mikel Delgado, a cat behavior consultant and Ph.D. student at UC-Berkeley, where she is studying psychology. In her work as a behavior consultant, she visits people's homes, where she sees what people aren't even realizing what they're not providing for their feline companions—and these are people, presumably, who have both the interest and the means in providing the best lives possible for their cats, given that they, you know, called a cat-behavior consultant. "I don't think most people neglect their pets' welfare intentionally," Delgado said. "I think with cats, there's this thought that they're low-maintenance pets." If only.

Cats—even older cats, even lazy cats—want, and need, to play, mimicking the hunting behaviors that come natural to them. And most of them need *you* to play *with* them, instead of "just leaving a bunch of ping-pong balls and mice toys lying around," Delgado says. She recommends one of those string-and-feathers-on-a-stick toys, which you can move around—slowly, mind you, or else the cat can't focus his eyes on it—waiting for them to pounce. (A cat that keeps you up at night, Delgado told me, is likely a cat that hasn't gotten enough exercise during the day.)

Additionally, it would benefit both cats and dogs if you made them work for their food, with the use of food puzzles (Kongs, for example). "When we brought them into our homes we provided all their food at once—we took away one of the biggest things they used their brains for, which is to get food," Delgado said. Social enrichment is a big deal for pets, too, and taking the time to play with them is one important way to provide that for them. For dogs, interaction with other dogs—say, at the dog park—is crucial, too, advises Marc Bekoff, an animal cognition researcher. (There is of course so, so much more to enrichment for pets; I'd recommend starting with Pierce's book if you want to know more.)

Pierce's intention isn't to condemn pet owners, but if she's made them feel guilty—well, good. Investigate that feeling, she urges, and understand that pet ownership isn't something to be taken lightly. Our animals make our lives so happy; it's the least we can do for them in return.

4

Avoid Puppy Mills and Backyard Breeders When Getting a Pet Dog or Cat

Paws, Inc.

Paws, Inc. is an organization of people dedicated to helping animals by caring for homeless, orphaned, or injured animals.

Getting a pet dog or cat can be an exciting and joyful experience, but buyers need to be aware of their new pet's background. According to some sources, a substantial portion of pets sold to the public come from puppy mills or backyard breeders. These pets, animal activists warn, are often seen as "cash crops," and are therefore neglected and mistreated. Being informed, asking questions, finding reputable breeders, and adopting rescued animals are the solutions to this problem and can help prevent buyers from unwittingly supporting puppy mills and cruel breeding practices.

Choosing to bring a new canine companion into your life is an exciting but involved decision-making process, especially when deciding where to get one. You might have concerns about "puppy mills" or "backyard breeders," and want to know how to steer clear of them. Perhaps you don't even know what these are and need more information.

As you begin your research, here are some things to consider:

"Buyer Beware: The Problem with Puppy Mills and Backyard Breeders," Paws, Inc. Reprinted by permission.

Puppy Mills

Puppy mills are commercial breeding facilities that mass-produce dogs (and cats in cat mills) for sale through pet stores, or directly to consumers through classified ads or the Internet. Roughly 90 percent of puppies in pet stores come from puppy mills. Many retailers who buy animals from such facilities take the wholesaler's word that the animals are happy and healthy without seeing for themselves.

In most states, these commercial breeding kennels can legally keep hundreds of dogs in cages their entire lives, for the sole purpose of continuously churning out puppies. The animals produced range from purebreds to any number of the latest "designer" mixed breeds. Cat breeding occurs under similar conditions to supply pet stores with kittens.

Animals in Puppy Mills Are Treated Like Cash Crops

- They are confined to squalid, overcrowded cages with minimal shelter from extreme weather and no choice but to sit and sleep in their own excrement.
- Animals suffer from malnutrition or starvation due to inadequate or unsanitary food and water.
- Sick or dying animals receive little or no veterinary care.
- Adult animals are continuously bred until they can no longer produce, then destroyed or discarded.
- Kittens and puppies are taken from their mothers at such an early age; many suffer from serious behavior problems.

Backyard Breeders

Backyard breeders are also motivated by profit. Ads from these unscrupulous breeders fill the classifieds. Backyard breeders may appear to be the nice neighbor next door—in fact, even seemingly good-intentioned breeders may treat their breeding pairs as family pets. However, continuously breeding animals for years to produce litters for a profit still jeopardizes the animals' welfare.

Some backyard breeders may only breed their family dog once in awhile, but they often are not knowledgeable on how to breed responsibly, such as screening for genetic defects. Responsible, proper breeding entails much more than simply putting two dogs together.

Look for These Red Flags

- The seller has many types of purebreds or "designer" hybrid breeds being sold at less than six weeks old.
- Breeders who are reluctant to show potential customers the entire premises on which animals are being bred and kept.
- Breeders who don't ask a lot of questions of potential buyers.
- No guarantees—responsible breeders make a commitment to take back the pet at anytime during the animal's life, no matter the reason.

Because puppy mills and backyard breeders choose profit over animal welfare, their animals typically do not receive proper veterinary care. Animals may seem healthy at first but later show issues like congenital eye and hip defects, parasites or even the deadly Parvovirus.

Taking Homes Away

When puppy mills and backyard breeders flood the market with animals, they reduce homes available for animals from reputable establishments, shelters and rescue groups. Every year, more than 150,000 cats and dogs enter shelters in Washington State—6 to 8 million animals enter shelters nationwide. Sadly, only about 15 percent of people with pets in the US adopted them from a shelter or rescue group, leaving so many deserving pets left behind.

Help Stop the Suffering by Taking These Steps

1. Be a responsible, informed consumer—if you do buy from a breeder, go to a reputable one who:

- Will show you where the dogs spend their time and introduces you to the puppy's parents.
- Explains the puppy's medical history, including vaccines, and gives you their veterinarian's contact info.
- Doesn't have puppies available year-round, yet may keep a waiting list for interested people.
- Asks about your family's lifestyle, why you want a dog, and your care and training plans for the puppy.
- Doesn't use pressure sales tactics.

2. Adopt from a shelter or breed-specific rescue group near you—typically 25% of the animals in shelters are purebred.

3. Support laws that protect animals from puppy mill cruelty—tell your elected officials you support laws which cap the number of animals a person can own and breed, and establish care standards for exercise, housing, access to food and water and regular veterinary care.

4. Urge your local pet store to support shelters—animals are often used to draw consumers into stores. Encourage pet stores to promote shelter animals for adoption instead of replenishing their supply through questionable sources.

5. Donate pet supplies to local shelters to help those rescued from the puppy mills and many other homeless animals in need.

6. Learn more at:

- CAPS-web.org (Companion Animal Protection Society)
- No Pet Store Puppies (ASPCA)
- PrisonersOfGreed.org
- StopPuppyMills.com (The Humane Society of the United States)

5

For Many Reasons, People Should No Longer Keep Pets

Linda Rodriguez McRobbie

Linda Rodriguez McRobbie is an American freelance journalist currently residing in London.

There are many reasons why some argue that animals should no longer be kept as pets. Research has shown that animals have more complex inner lives than we had initially anticipated, and as pets that are completely in our care, animals have almost no control over their own lives. Many countries are enacting laws that serve to protect animals and pets from abusive and negligent owners. Additionally, institutions that exploit animals, such as circuses, are more frequently being shut down.

I t was a Tupperware tub of live baby rats that made Dr. Jessica Pierce start to question the idea of pet ownership. She was at her local branch of PetSmart, a pet store chain in the US, buying crickets for her daughter's gecko. The baby rats, squeaking in their plastic container, were brought in by a man she believed was offering to sell them to the store as pets or as food for the resident snakes. She didn't ask. But Pierce, a bioethicist, was troubled.

"Rats have a sense of empathy and there has been a lot of research on what happens when you take babies away from a

"Should We Stop Keeping Pets? Why More and More Ethicists Say Yes," by Linda Rodriguez McRobbie, Guardian News and Media Limited, August 1, 2017. Reprinted by permission.

mother rat—not surprisingly, they experience profound distress," she says. "It was a slap in the face—how can we do this to animals?"

Pierce went on to write *Run, Spot, Run,* which outlines the case against pet ownership, in 2015. From the animals that become dog and cat food and the puppy farms churning out increasingly unhealthy purebred canines, to the goldfish sold by the bag and the crickets by the box, pet ownership is problematic because it denies animals the right of self-determination. Ultimately, we bring them into our lives because we want them, then we dictate what they eat, where they live, how they behave, how they look, even whether they get to keep their sex organs.

Treating animals as commodities isn't new or shocking; humans have been meat-eaters and animal-skin-wearers for millennia. However, this is at odds with how we say we feel about our pets. The British pet industry is worth about £10.6bn; Americans spent more than $66bn (£50bn) on their pets in 2016. A survey earlier this year found that many British pet owners love their pet more than they love their partner (12%), their children (9%) or their best friend (24%). According to another study, 90% of pet-owning Britons think of their pet as a member of their family, with 16% listing their animals in the 2011 census.

"It is morally problematic, because more people are thinking of pets as people … They consider them part of their family, they think of them as their best friend, they wouldn't sell them for a million dollars," says Dr. Hal Herzog, a professor of psychology at Western Carolina University and one of the founders of the budding field of anthrozoology, which examines human-animal relations. At the same time, research is revealing that the emotional lives of animals, even relatively "simple" animals such as goldfish, are far more complex and rich than we once thought ("dogs are people, too", according to a 2013 *New York Times* comment piece by the neuroscientist Gregory Berns). "The logical consequence is that the more we attribute them with these characteristics, the less right we have to control every single aspect of their lives," says Herzog.

Does this mean that, in 50 years or 100 years, we won't have pets? Institutions that exploit animals, such as the circus, are shutting down – animal rights activists claimed a significant victory this year with the closure of Ringling Bros. circus—and there are calls to end, or at least rethink, zoos. Meanwhile, the number of Britons who profess to be vegan is on the rise, skyrocketing 350% between 2006 and 2016.

Widespread petkeeping is a relatively recent phenomenon. Until the 19th century, most animals owned by households were working animals that lived alongside humans and were regarded unsentimentally. In 1698, for example, a Dorset farmer recorded in his diary: "My old dog Quon was killed and baked for his grease, which yielded 11lb." However, in the 19th and 20th centuries, animals began to feature less in our increasingly urban environments and, as disposable income grew, pets became more desirable. Even as people began to dote on their pets, though, animal life was not attributed any intrinsic value. In *Run, Spot, Run,* Pierce reports that, in 1877, the city of New York rounded up 762 stray dogs and drowned them in the East River, shoving them into iron crates and lifting the crates by crane into the water. Veterinarian turned philosopher Bernard Rollin recalls pet owners in the 1960s putting their dog to sleep before going on holiday, reasoning that it was cheaper to get a new dog when they returned than to board the one they had.

More recently, however, several countries have moved to change the legal status of animals. In 2015, the government of New Zealand recognised animals as sentient beings, in effect declaring them no longer property (how this squares with New Zealand's recent "war on possums" is unclear), as did the Canadian province of Quebec. While pets remain property in the UK, the Animal Welfare Act of 2006 stipulates that pet owners must provide a basic level of care for their animals. Pets are also property in the US, but 32 states, as well as Puerto Rico and Washington, DC, now include provisions for pets under domestic violence protection orders. In 2001, Rhode Island changed its legislation to describe pet owners as "guardians," a move that some animal rights' advocates lauded (and others criticised for being nothing more than a change in name).

Before we congratulate ourselves on how far we have come, consider that 1.5m shelter animals—including 670,000 dogs and 860,000 cats—are euthanised each year in the US. The number of stray dogs euthanised annually in the UK is far lower—3,463—but the RSCPA says investigations into animal cruelty cases increased 5% year on year in 2016, to 400 calls a day.

"Can I stick my dog in a car and take him to the vet and say: 'I don't want him any more, kill him,' or take him to a city shelter and say: 'I can't keep him any more, I hope you can find a home for him, good luck'?" says Gary Francione, a professor at Rutgers Law School in New Jersey and an animal rights advocate. "If you can still do that, if you still have the right to do that, then they are still property."

Crucially, our animals can't tell us whether they are happy being pets. "There is an illusion now that pets have more voice than in the past … but it is maybe more that we are putting words into their mouth," Pierce says, pointing to the abundance of pets on social media plastered with witty projections written by their "parents." "Maybe we are humanising them in a way that actually makes them invisible."

If you accept the argument that pet ownership is morally questionable, how do you put the brakes on such a vast industry? While he was writing his 2010 book, *Some We Love, Some We Hate, Some We Eat*, Herzog was studying the motivations of animal rights activists and whether it was emotion or intellect that pushed them towards activism. One of the subjects, Herzog says, was "very, very logical." After he had become a vegan, eschewed leather shoes and convinced his girlfriend to go vegan, he considered his pet cockatiel. "I remember; he looked up wistfully. He said he got the bird, took it outside, let it loose and it flew up," Herzog recalls. "He said: 'I knew she wouldn't survive, that she probably starved. I guess I was doing it more for myself than for her.'"

Although Pierce and Francione agree that pet ownership is wrong, both of them have pets: Pierce has two dogs and a cat; Francione has six rescue dogs, whom he considers "refugees." For now, the argument over whether we should own animals is largely theoretical: we *do* have pets and giving them up might cause more harm than good. Moreover, as Francione suggests, caring for pets seems to many people to be the one area where we can actually do right by animals; convincing people of the opposite is a hard sell.

Tim Wass, the chair of the Pet Charity, an animal welfare consultant and a former chief officer at the RSPCA, agrees. "It has already been decided by market forces and human nature … the reality is people have pets in the millions. The question is: how can we help them care for them correctly and appropriately?"

If the short history of pet ownership tells us anything, it is that our attitude towards animals is prone to change. "You see these rises and falls in our relationships with pets," says Herzog. "In the long haul, I think petkeeping might fall out of fashion; I think it is possible that robots will take their place, or maybe pet owning will be for small numbers of people. Cultural trends come and go. The more we think of pets as people, the less ethical it is to keep them."

6

Poaching and the Illegal Wildlife Trade Must Be Stopped

US Department of State

The US State Department is a branch of the United States government. One of the agency's responsibilities is to stem wildlife trafficking and stop poaching.

Will future generations of people ever get to see majestic wild animals that are currently endangered? Unless poaching and the illegal wildlife trade are stopped, elephants, rhinos, tigers, exotic birds, and many other creatures are in danger of disappearing from the wild. The US has implemented a plan to thwart efforts of poachers and other criminals that engage in the trade of wild animals. With laws enacted within the country and trade agreements and policies with other nations, the United States is making a great effort to curtail this scourge on wildlife.

D id you ever get to see an elephant in the wild before they became extinct?" This is a question children may soon be asking unless we take immediate action. Wildlife trafficking—not just of elephants, but also of rhinos, tigers, great apes, exotic birds, and many other species—has exploded in recent years to become a multibillion-dollar criminal enterprise with increasingly grave and potentially irreversible consequences. The scourge of wildlife trafficking threatens conservation efforts, national security, the

"A Roadmap to Fighting Poaching and Illegal Wildlife Trade," US Department of State.

rule of law, regional stability, and the sustainable livelihoods of communities. So what are we doing to stop this problem?

Today, the United States launched an Implementation Plan for the President's National Strategy for Combating Wildlife Trafficking, which will be a roadmap to fighting poaching and illegal wildlife trade. The plan focuses on three key areas: strengthening law enforcement domestically and globally, reducing demand, and building international cooperation. Wildlife trafficking is a global problem that demands a global solution. We are determined to be a part of that solution, and we will continue to work closely in our efforts with foreign governments, non-governmental organizations, the private sector, community leaders, and civil society to achieve this goal.

Strong law enforcement is critical to stopping criminals engaged in wildlife crime. The US Department of Justice has indicted, prosecuted, and secured convictions in numerous cases of trafficking in internationally protected species, such as elephant ivory, rhinoceros horn, narwhal tusk, turtles, and reptiles. Investigative efforts led by the US Fish and Wildlife Service targeted traffickers in rhinoceros horn, elephant ivory, and other wildlife products, concentrating on organized smuggling rings, middlemen, and art and antique dealers. Operation Crash—named after the collective term for a herd of rhinoceros—has led to significant prison terms and fines for those involved, as well as the forfeiture of millions of dollars in cash, gold bars, rhino horn, and luxury vehicles and jewelry.

To respond effectively to wildlife trafficking, most countries need to enact more robust laws while enhancing their investigative, law enforcement, and judicial capacity to stem the corruption and illicit flow of money associated with wildlife trafficking. In 2014, the Department of State's capacity-building efforts centered on training programs for our foreign counterparts in Southeast Asia, Africa, and Central and South America, strengthening national legislative, investigative, prosecutorial, and judicial processes to enforce wildlife laws. The Department of State supported approximately

20 training programs across the law enforcement spectrum, helping more than 30 countries combat wildlife trafficking more effectively. The programs also provided an opportunity to improve international cooperation on wildlife trafficking investigations, since this international threat requires a transnational response.

Many Americans are surprised to learn that our nation ranks among the highest in the consumption of wildlife and wildlife products, both legal and illegal. To demonstrate global leadership and limit opportunities open to traffickers in the United States, we have begun tightening domestic regulations around the trade in wildlife, and elevated awareness of the plight of elephants, rhinos and other highly trafficked species in an effort to curtail demand. In 2014, the Fish and Wildlife Service banned all commercial imports of ivory into the United States, and will propose a near complete ban on trade in ivory within the United States this year.

And we destroyed six tons of ivory taken in law enforcement raids and seizures over the past 20 years to send a global message that ivory must be rendered valueless as a commodity and the trade in elephant ivory crushed.

Building on these efforts, we will continue to take measures in the United States to enhance our own law enforcement capabilities while supporting foreign governments with technical assistance, training, and analytical tools to build their capacity. We will also use diplomatic cooperation tools, such as the UN Convention against Transnational Organized Crime, to bolster international action on combating wildlife trafficking.

Decreasing demand for illegal wildlife and wildlife products is critical. In cooperation with our partners, we will continue to raise public awareness of the harmful impact from these purchases through public service announcements, media campaigns, and community outreach. We will work with the tourism and transportation sectors, including airlines, hotel chains, restaurants and online retailers to support their commitment to halt the sale of illegal wildlife and wildlife products. We will encourage foreign governments and corporations in major consumer countries to lead by example and eliminate illegal wildlife and wildlife products from official functions while strengthening local policies and enforcement.

Our diplomatic engagement on this issue is at the highest levels of government, and coordinated on-the-ground efforts. While we aim to take the profit out of wildlife crime and increase the risks for its perpetrators, we are also fully committed to helping people in wildlife/biodiversity hotspots by strengthening social and economic incentives in their communities to protect wildlife. To be successful, conservation efforts must benefit both wildlife and the people who share an ecosystem. To cite just one key example, wild elephant populations generate orders of magnitude more in revenue to local economies from tourism than they ever can from the illegal sale of their ivory.

Many protected and endangered species faced a difficult year in 2014. Elephants reached a dangerous tipping point with an average of more than 20,000 African elephants killed per year since 2010. Pangolins, which are found in tropical areas in Asia and Africa and closely resemble a scaly anteater, are now the most trafficked species to date. A record number of rhinos were killed in South Africa last year, with 1,215 animals poached in 2014 alone. Despite this grim picture, there is still reason for hope. When the Chinese government joined international efforts to end the consumption of shark fin soup—which has contributed to the deaths of some 70 million sharks each year—by banning its consumption at state dinners, shark fin sales reportedly dropped by 50–70 percent. This demonstrates that progress is possible when governments take action, civil society raises awareness, and companies refuse to support wildlife trafficking.

We are also using trade agreements and trade policy to press for groundbreaking commitments on wildlife trafficking and wildlife conservation in the Trans-Pacific Partnership Agreement (TPP) with eleven other countries in the Asia-Pacific region and the Transatlantic Partnership Agreement (T-TIP) with the European Union (EU). These commitments would be fully enforceable, including through recourse to trade sanctions, with far-reaching benefits for species like rhinos, sharks, and pangolins.

Given the enormous consequences of the scourge of wildlife trafficking, we all have a moral obligation to fight it. Future generations are relying on us to take on a leadership role and act now.

7

Puppy Mills Are Puppy Breeding Prisons

American Society for the Prevention of Cruelty to Animals

The American Society for the Prevention of Cruelty to Animals (ASPCA) was founded in 1866 as the first humane society in the United States. Today it is dedicated to the prevention of cruelty to animals and animal rights.

This viewpoint argues that puppy mill breeders are generally only concerned with maximizing profits by producing a continuous stream of puppies to sell. Consequently, breeders keep adult dogs in poor living conditions to cut costs, yet expect the dogs to keep producing litters of pups. When the dogs can no longer have puppies they are often killed. The puppies may also experience hardships such as fear and loneliness before they are sold and transported to pet shops. This viewpoint discusses the conditions typically found in puppy mills to persuade readers against patronizing them.

L ike you, we love dogs. They're members of the family—often our favorite members! But too many dogs in America don't know this kind of love. Victims of the high-volume puppy industry, they're bred for profit and kept in tiny, filthy cages. These dogs don't receive any affection, exercise or proper veterinary care. And when they can no longer produce puppies, they are discarded.

"A Closer Look at Puppy Mills," American Society for the Prevention of Cruelty to Animals. Reprinted by permission.

Learn how this shadowy industry uses sophisticated but dishonest techniques to market its adorable "product."

The Hallmarks of Cruel Breeding

Cruel commercial breeders want to maximize profit by producing a high number of puppies at the lowest possible cost. Here's how they do it.

Tiny Cages

More adult dogs to breed equals more puppies, which equals more money, so cruel breeders maximize space by keeping mother and father dogs tightly contained. They're often kept in ramshackle outdoor pens, exposed to the elements, or in tiny, filthy cages for their entire lives. Caged dogs develop lesions and sores from constantly standing on uncomfortable wire flooring, and can get cut on the wire's sharp points. Because the cages are usually stacked vertically, urine and feces rain down onto the dogs below. Dogs of all ages and sizes may be crammed in together, which can lead to stress, aggression and fighting. They aren't taken on walks, and don't get to play with toys or run around. They eat, sleep, relieve themselves and give birth in these cages. It's the only reality they'll ever know.

Poor Veterinary Care and Hygiene

Dogs, like people, need regular health care. However, health care can be costly, so dogs in cruel breeding facilities aren't typically cared for by a veterinarian—not for vaccines, not for regular checkups, not when they're sick and not for a teeth cleaning. Since breeding dogs aren't seen by the public, they aren't bathed and their hair is not brushed or cut. These dogs are left to suffer through painful injuries, broken bones, rotting teeth, dangerous levels of filth, festering mats that pull at their skin, and nails so long that they curl back into and pierce their paw pads.

The filthy conditions found in these facilities encourage the spread of diseases, especially among puppies with immature immune systems. Sometimes these illnesses can be life-threatening, painful and expensive to treat. Puppies often arrive in pet stores with health issues ranging from parasites to parvo to pneumonia. Because puppies are removed from their littermates and mothers at a very young age, they also can suffer from fear, anxiety and other lasting behavioral problems. Sometimes these issues don't show up until people bring the puppy home, only to be confronted with unpredictable, expensive and oftentimes chronic medical problems.

Nonstop Breeding

Female dogs are treated like puppy-making machines. They are bred at every opportunity, without any rest time between litters, and when their bodies are so depleted that they can no longer produce puppies, they're often abandoned or killed. The puppies are the lucky ones—they usually leave these horrible conditions by the time they're eight weeks old. The parents of these puppies, however, are unlikely to make it out alive. Their only job is to produce puppies for as long as they live.

Disregard for Genetics

All puppies are cute, and unless you are an expert it can be tough to notice the physical differences between them. Unfortunately, a lot of serious medical and behavioral problems don't reveal themselves until a puppy grows up—that's why careful breeding is so important. Because quality is not a priority for cruel breeders, they don't bother to remove medically compromised dogs from their breeding stock, resulting in generation after generation of dogs with unchecked hereditary defects. These frequently include heart disease, deafness, bone disorders like hip dysplasia, and blood and respiratory disorders.

How Cruel Breeding Hurts Dogs

Dogs imprisoned in puppy mills often suffer from extreme physical and emotional problems—as do their puppies, in ways you can and cannot see.

There's a reason the puppy mill industry doesn't show you where their puppies come from. To turn a profit, corners need to be cut, and it's the dogs imprisoned in puppy mills who pay the price both physically and emotionally.

Puppies born into this sad world are comparatively lucky in one way: because they need to be sold while they're small and young, the time they spend in these facilities is brief. Unfortunately, the effects of where and how they were bred last a lifetime. Poor genetics, early weaning, unsanitary environments and significant stress can contribute to the development of serious health and behavioral problems that are expensive, difficult or impossible to treat.

Constant Fear and Stress

Lack of normal human interaction hurts typically social animals like dogs. Dogs kept in commercial breeding facilities may pace back and forth in their cages, bark nonstop, cower or appear entirely shut down. Since puppy mills only plan on selling puppies, there is little incentive to provide much physical or emotional care to the adult breeding dogs.

Set Up for Failure

Cruel breeders want to produce as many puppies as possible as quickly as possible. Unlike responsible breeders, they don't screen for inheritable disorders and remove dogs from their breeding program who are less likely to produce healthy puppies. Even psychological issues like anxiety and fearfulness can have genetic roots. And it only makes sense that, just like with humans, an unborn baby might be affected by a mother's stress: Stressful puppy mill conditions that hurt mom, which include being bred constantly without any rest time, can potentially also harm her puppies.

Sudden Separation

The first months of puppies' lives are a critical socialization period. Spending that time with their mother and littermates, along with slow weaning, helps prevent problems like extreme shyness, aggression, fear and anxiety. But puppies born in puppy mills are usually removed abruptly from their littermates and mothers at very early ages. This can cause underdevelopment and long-lasting emotional and behavior problems.

Alone in a Crowd

Puppies from cruel breeders are often shipped, typically by truck and sometimes over long distances, to brokers and eventually to pet stores. Puppies might also be shipped by plane. The transport is noisy, may be too hot or cold, and smells of other dogs and their comingled waste. The young puppy is now housed with unrelated dogs in an unfamiliar place without his mother or littermates. He might feel hungry, thirsty, scared or sick. The puppy can be exposed to illness and disease. At the pet store, the puppy is again put into new, unfamiliar surroundings and handled by many different people. This is not a promising way to start a new life.

The Puppy Pipeline

Who gets the puppies from the breeders to the pet stores? Between points A and B, there's a lesser-known side industry at work that perpetuates and profits from animal cruelty.

Cruel puppy breeders rely on pet shops and online retailers to present a spotless, happy image so customers won't think about where puppies are born and how their parents are treated. But there are also other industries that make the puppy pipeline possible, including dog brokers, auctions, and transporters.

Dog Brokers

Do you ever wonder how a pet store can have such a variety of different puppy breeds available at the same time? It would seemingly be difficult for a local pet store to keep track of many breeders and when they have puppies available in order to fill their shop with the right assortment to match customers' desires at any given time. Dog brokers help solve this problem.

A dog broker or puppy dealer is a middleman, a distributor who obtains puppies en masse from commercial breeders and re-sells them to retailers. They offer one-stop shopping for pet stores, and make it easy for them to offer the array of puppies customers want. There are currently about 300 USDA-licensed puppy brokers in the United States. There is no knowing how many people are doing this work unlicensed.

Breeders are happy to work with brokers because many brokers will buy in bulk. Brokers might take all the puppies a breeder has available—even ones a breeder would have a hard time selling on their own—and are willing to truck puppies over long distances to their final retail destinations.

Since cruel breeders have increasingly turned to the Internet to sell puppies, some brokers now sell directly to the public. They might call themselves "puppy finders" or "puppy concierges." Instead of physically buying and then re-selling puppies, these brokers create fancy websites and customer service platforms, making "matches" between their database of breeders and the unwitting online customer.

Transporters

Commercial breeders and brokers can be found anywhere, but tend to be most concentrated in certain parts of the US. (Ohio, Missouri, Indiana have some of the highest numbers of USDA-licensed breeders). To get their puppies to stores around the country, breeders rely not only on brokers; they sometimes use other transporters. These could be transporters whose main business is moving puppies, or carriers who are willing to transport puppies in addition to other products.

Although there are some standards in place for the commercial transport of puppies, they, like the requirements for commercial breeders, are minimal and poorly enforced. There is no limit to the number of continuous hours puppies may be trucked, or how many animals may be packed into one vehicle. The transporters need to offer food or water to a young puppy only once every 12 hours. There is no requirement that the driver have any animal care experience. Crowded conditions on a truck for hours or days can significantly stress a very young puppy, result in disease transmission, or worse: In 2016, more than 50 puppies died in

Missouri when a driver allowed the inside of a transport vehicle to overheat. Sadly, the tragic stories don't stop there.

Auctions

Commercial breeders often buy and sell dogs with other breeders if they want to add new breeds to their business or get rid of dogs they no longer want. Auction services allow many dog breeders to meet under one roof, where hundreds of dogs are displayed and sold to the highest bidder. The auction house gets a cut of the profit.

For some breeding dogs, the trip to the dog auction is the only time they ever get to leave the cages in which they've spent their entire lives. But if they get sold, it just means a trip to a different cage. Dogs who fail to attract bidders could be discarded or abandoned by their owners, since they no longer have any perceived value.

8

Finding a Good Dog Breeder Is Possible

Your Dog's Friend

Your Dog's Friend is a nonprofit organization dedicated to educating dog owners and keeping dogs out of shelters.

Unlike puppy mills, the organization Your Dog's Friend argues that it actually is possible to find breeders that treat their dogs in an ethical manner. There are ways to determine if a dog breeder is genuinely concerned for dogs and interested in raising healthy animals instead of simply churning out puppies for profit. After locating a possible breeder, there are certain ways to determine if the breeder is legitimate. This viewpoint outlines the steps for finding a good breeder who supports the proper treatment of dogs.

A fter taking a realistic look at your lifestyle and resources, you are ready to start searching for YOUR DOG. Although you know that many wonderful canines—both "Heinz 57" and purebreds—are available for adoption, you decide to look into purchasing a pup or older dog.

That Doggie in the Window (or Website)

Pet stores do not want people to realize that at least 95% of the "merchandise" is born in puppy mills, infamous for the cruel treatment of dogs. Purchasers of puppy-mill pups often pay a very high price both financially and emotionally when they discover

"Breeders vs. Puppy Mills: How to Find A Good Breeder," Your Dog's Friend. Reprinted by permission.

their new pet comes to them with an illness or congenital defect. The smart consumer will boycott any pet store that sells puppies— both small family-owned stores and large chains. As of April 2011, federal law still does not require any breeder that sells directly to the public—over the Internet or otherwise—to be inspected to ensure that breeder dogs are cared for humanely. Puppy millers will continue to take advantage of this until Congress closes the loophole. If you decide to buy a dog directly from a breeder, limit your search to breeders within driving distance. The only way to be absolutely certain that the parents of your prospective puppy are healthy, socialized and well cared for is to see the breeder's home and dogs yourself.

The Search

Look for a breed fancier with lots of experience and a breeding plan that stresses health, temperament and socialization. The best way to find a breeder is to be on the lookout for a wonderful dog, and then ask the owner where s/he got the pet. Other good strategies are to:

- Go to performance events like agility and rally. While you are there, talk to handlers and owners. Just make sure they have time to give you and are not preparing to compete.
- Consult web sites and publications of national registries and parent clubs. (Warning: Listing is not necessarily an endorsement by an organization.)
- Get advice from vets, groomers, and members of local training clubs and kennel clubs.

The Selection Process

A reputable breeder wants to cover expenses—not make her living selling dogs. Do not deal with anyone who breeds more than two breeds or specializes in rare colors, sizes, etc. Eliminate from your list any breeder who only accepts cash or credit cards. A breeder should encourage you to visit—not ask to meet you someplace "convenient" to exchange money and pup. Cross a breeder off your list if you find dirty conditions. Frightened, antisocial or unhealthy-looking dogs on the premises are serious deal breakers. Never buy a dog from anyone who does not want you to visit their home and spend some time with their dogs. Make sure you meet at least one parent of the litter. If you want an older dog that is already trained, housebroken, and socialized, the breeder might have one available that you can get to know on a visit before any decision is made.

While you are with the breeder, take a look at available background documentation—for example, health records and litter registration. Ask for referrals from a vet, local breed club, or satisfied puppy buyers. Question the breeder about her experience and breeding plan. Discuss the breeder's views on socialization and early neurological stimulation.

Make sure any breeder you deal with:

- Screens pups for genetic problems and shows you the paperwork;
- Answers questions with no hesitation or condescension;
- Takes the time to educate you and does not push the sale;
- Helps you make the right decision—even if that means you do not buy a dog; and
- Agrees to provide advice and support for the dog's lifetime if you do buy a dog.

A good breeder will often have a puppy waiting list and always interrogates potential buyers about their ability to care for the dog. Questions the breeder will probably ask include:

- Why do you want a dog?
- Who will be responsible for the dog's care and exercise?
- Do you have a fenced yard? (Some breeders may actually want to visit your home.)
- If you rent your home, can I contact your landlord to make sure dogs are allowed?

- What veterinarian have you used in the past so I can call for a reference?

The Deal

The price of a pet-quality puppy varies based on the breed, but typically ranges from $400 to $2000. For example, one Doberman pinscher fancier estimates that the cost per puppy in a litter is over $1600 when the breeder is doing "all the right things" (health testing, ear docking, vaccinations, vet care, supplies, etc.). Good breeders deserve to be compensated for the time and resources they put into producing sound pups.

The Contract

A reputable breeder's goal is that every pup bred is healthy and will make someone a fine companion. Keep in mind, however, that some pups in a litter will match the breed standard more than others. Pups identified as potentially competitive in conformation shows are considered show quality; others are pet quality; and some pups may take the breeder longer than the first few weeks to evaluate. When a dog that is (or might be) show quality is sold to a "pet" home, a breeder may want to retain some control just in case the dog might be of use to the breeder in the future. For example, the contract might include language that requires a buyer to get the breeder's permission before the dog can be neutered; or a co-ownership provision might oblige the owner to return the dog temporarily to the breeder, at the owner's expense, for breeding or training. If you want to be the only one with decision-making power over your dog, then read the contract carefully before you sign it.

A straight-forward pet quality contract should include the buyer's promise to spay or neuter the dog as well as a health/ wellness guarantee from the breeder. A valid American Kennel Club (AKC) Dog Registration Application form provided by the breeder simply allows the buyer to register the new pup. Registration does not guarantee anything at all about your new dog:

"*[A registration certificate] in no way indicates the quality or state of health of the dog ... Many people breed their dogs with no concern for the qualitative demands of the breed standards. When this occurs repeatedly over several generations, the animals, while still purebred, can be of extremely low quality. Before buying a dog, you should investigate the dog's parentage (including titles, DNA and pedigree information), the breeder's breeding practices, the breed standard, and the genetic tests recommended by the Parent Club for the breed.*"

– *"About Registration," from the AKC website*

Bottom line: Make sure the terms of the breeder's contract also protect you and your new dog!

Puppy Mills

Puppy mills are places where purebred or "designer" dogs are bred solely for the money they can bring in, with no regard for the dogs' welfare. The puppies are housed in overcrowded, unsanitary cages. Puppies are taken away from their mothers too early and are not socialized with either dogs or humans. They receive minimal, if any, veterinary care, and inbreeding is common. Disease, genetic disorders, and heartworm are the norm. The breeding females produce one litter after another in cramped cages with no concern for their health.

Puppy mill dogs are sold to pet stores and advertised on the internet and in newspapers. If you are told that a breeding facility is "USDA-licensed" or "USDA-inspected," that only means that minimal standards of food, water, and shelter have been met. It says nothing about meeting the needs or securing the welfare of the breeder's dogs. AKC registration papers also tell you nothing about the condition of the dog or how it was raised.

Reputable breeders want you to visit their facility. They ask a lot of questions in order to assess whether or not you will be a suitable and responsible parent for their puppies. Responsible breeders also don't churn out puppies as if from a factory. They generally have a waiting list because they have a limited number of litters born each year.

Those of you who have rescued puppy mill dogs know the difficulties these dogs can face. In addition to health issues, most have never been housetrained; have never walked on a solid surface or with a leash; have never lived in a home with vacuum cleaners, blenders and other appliances; have never climbed stairs; have never interacted normally with other dogs or people.

9

Puppy Mills, Past and Present

Ivy Collier

Ivy Collier is an independent researcher, animal advocate, and writer.

Puppy mills have been around for quite a while at this point. History shows that this unfortunate way of breeding dogs came into practice after World War II and continues to this day. Surprisingly, the US Department of Agriculture once promoted puppy milling as a profitable business. However, in more recent years, citizens and animal welfare groups have convinced lawmakers to enact laws requiring dog breeders to be licensed and inspected on a regular basis. This viewpoint explores the surprising history of puppy mills in the United States and current efforts to counteract them.

This blog examines puppy mills in the US. It explains what they are, how they came to be, the number that are in operation, and how many dogs are impacted. The piece also outlines some of the many problems with these facilities and explains how the new Puppy Uniform Protection and Safety Act (PUPS Act) can address the so-called "Internet loophole" in puppy sales.

What Are Puppy Mills?

Many people throughout the US have seen headlines plastered across newspapers or television screens, "Puppy Mill Bust" or "Puppy Mill Raid." But what exactly are puppy mills? At this time,

"The History of Puppy Mills and Why You Should Care," Ivy Collier, guest writer, *Faunalytics*, January 1, 2014. Reprinted by permission.

there is no standard definition of the term. However, the definition that I use is that puppy mills are "large usually filthy facilities that are usually found in rural areas, where puppies are bred in large numbers and usually sold to pet stores via brokers" (Williams & DeMello, 2007). According to the US Department of Agriculture (USDA) any breeder that owns more than three breeding female dogs and/or has gross sales over $500 per year is considered a commercial breeder. However, this definition regulates breeders that sell directly to pet stores but does *not* cover Internet sales to individuals. This allows breeders to breed and sell dogs in this manner without any federal oversight.

The History of Puppy Mills and Why You Should Care

Puppy mills came into popularity after World War II in reaction to crop failures in the Midwest. What may be hard to believe today is that the USDA actually promoted puppy mills by advertising that it was a lucrative and failproof business. Encouraged by the government, farmers started to pack dogs into chicken coops and rabbit hutches and sell puppies to pet stores.

Today, the USDA estimates that there are between 2,000–3,000 federally licensed commercial breeding facilities in the US with approximately 1,045 of these facilities being in Missouri (645), Iowa (237), and Kansas (178). The ASPCA believes there are close to 10,000 puppy mill breeders. However, the majority of these breeders are either not properly licensed or are not required to be licensed because they operate on a smaller scale. Since these breeders are not tracked by the USDA, it is nearly impossible to know exactly how many puppy mills are in the US. It is also close to impossible to learn exactly how many dogs are living in puppy mills as some breeders are not required to keep accurate records, or if the breeder is illegal, they will purposely not keep records. However, according to the Humane Society of the United States (HSUS), there is an estimated 176,088 dogs kept for breeding at USDA licensed facilities and approximately 1,075,896 puppies born in facilities each year. HSUS estimates that there is an estimated 2.15 million puppies that are sold each year. Many of these puppies are sold via the Internet where there is currently no USDA oversight. It is saddening to think about thousands upon thousands of dogs are living in small, dark, cramped cages for their entire lives and are refused even very basic veterinary care. The use of stacked, wire cages makes it difficult to avoid contact with urine, feces, and other infectious diseases due to the dogs' paws slipping through the wire and into the waste. Combined with the lack of grooming, environmental cleanliness and oversight, these dogs have a slim chance of living a healthy, happy life.

PUPS Act and the New Rule

Citizens and animal welfare organizations have worked for years to help these animals and some public officials are now listening. Congressman Jim Gerlach (PA), cosponsored by Congressman Sam Farr (CA) and supported by Senator Dick Durbin (IL), introduced a bill entitled the *Puppy Uniform Protection and Safety Act (PUPS Act)* on February 27, 2013. In essence, the PUPS Act closes the so-called "Internet loophole." Great! But what is the Internet loophole? The loophole consists of breeders that sell puppies via the Internet, mail, or by phone, and who are not subject to the same regulations that govern traditional breeders. This bill calls for high volume commercial breeders, which is any person who breeds more than four female dogs and sells the puppies online, by mail, or over the phone to be federally licensed and inspected on a regular basis in the same way as traditional commercial breeders. This bipartisan collaboration resulted in a new USDA rule that mirrors the PUPS Act. I contacted a staffer from Congressman Gerlach's office regarding the status of the PUPS Act and was told that he submitted a press release on September 10, 2013. Congressman Gerlach stated, "By closing this Internet loophole in the federal Animal Welfare Act), the law has finally caught up to technology. This action is long overdue and necessary to end the horrific conditions and inhumane treatment of dogs at large breeding kennels here in Pennsylvania and throughout the country."

Not everyone sees this new rule as progress; critics of the PUPS Act believe it is intrusive. Some say the term "high volume breeders" is too broad and can potentially affect smaller breeders that have four or less breeding dogs. There are also concerns about the fees and inspections that small breeders would now be subject to. A number of small breeders feel that these restrictions can hamper the sport of breeding and possibly the advancement of certain breeds.

Conversely, many animal advocates are pleased with the new rule or at least believe it is a step in the right direction. Hopefully, this will help thousands of dogs suffering in puppy mills see a brighter day.

10

Animal Shelters: To Kill or Not to Kill?

Julie Zack Yaste

Julie Zack Yaste is a freelance writer and editor.

Sick, abandoned, lost, or poorly tamed animals—these are all types that could potentially end up in an animal shelter. But what happens next to these creatures? Basically, there are two types of animal shelters: "kill" and "no-kill." Both types of shelters have their own rules and procedures, but both try to keep their shelter residents healthy and content and get them adopted into new homes. Shelter staff have a big responsibility and often must make do with little funding. This viewpoint discusses the two types of shelters and the advantages and disadvantages of both.

People don't usually become involved with animal shelters unless they are passionate about animal welfare. But there are different ideas out there about how to promote best the mission of improving animal lives.

Unfortunately, the rhetoric surrounding animal shelters galvanizes controversy and divides the community. Shelters often are categorized as "kill" or "no-kill." Using such emotionally charged language as the baseline for distinguishing different types of shelters is a gross miscarriage of justice. It simultaneously demonizes one type of establishment and deifies another, without delving into the major complexities involved in each.

"Kill vs. No-Kill Shelters: The Great Debate," by Julie Zack Yaste, Waylon H. Lewis Enterprises, September 8, 2015. Originally published on elephantjournal.com. Reprinted by permission.

Although circumstances vary, usually "no kill" shelters are closed admission. That means they are not required to accept every animal presented. Animals that clearly have life-threatening ailments, or those that are definitively not capable of rehabilitation can be turned away. The sad repercussions of "no kill" shelters that have a zero-euthanasia policy are that they will deny admittance to terminally ill animals, or allow terminally ill animals to endure until they are adopted or expire. Either way, the animal suffers.

On the other hand, "kill" shelters, are often open admission. They will take any animal regardless of its health condition (including the terminally ill) or the likelihood of rehabilitation.

Open admissions shelters break down into two categories:

1. Shelters that regularly euthanize healthy, adoptable animals to make room.

2. Shelters that will make every effort not to euthanize any healthy, adoptable animals.

It is an important distinction to make, as many people assume that all shelters that euthanize animals have a proverbial "sell-by" date. What this means, is if the animal has not been adopted by a certain date it will automatically be put down. It is true that this happens in some shelters, notably under-funded local government facilities.

There are, however, open admissions shelters that will only euthanize an adoptable animal for space under the direst circumstances. I've seen shelters that kept animals for months, even over a year in one case, in an attempt to place the animal in the right home. The main problem I find with open admissions animal shelters is that there does have to be a decision point where someone evaluates whether or not an animal could be adopted.

The criteria for adoptability includes health and temperament. Health seems like it should be straightforward. If an animal isn't critically or terminally ill it is nursed to good health and adopted into a forever home, right? Wrong. Unfortunately, there's often somewhat of a cost-benefit analysis associated with ailments and ability to provide care. Frequently certain ailments, such as some cancers, can cause an animal to be automatically euthanized.

Fortunately, there are funds that sometimes go towards extensive animal rehabilitation at specified shelters. For example, at the Hawaiian Humane Society, there is Max's Fund, dedicated to providing intensive care outside of what shelter clinic staff can provide. This fund has been used for amputating unsalvageable limbs or other major surgeries that could not otherwise be provided. Without the fund, countless animals would not currently be alive much less thriving in new homes.

However, not all shelters have this kind of resource, though. Many animal shelters are drastically under-funded, and simply do not have the resources to provide all of the life-saving care needed to help animals get adopted.

Once an animal has passed a health screening, it is further screened for temperament. Sometimes this is an easy process. Dogs that have a history of aggression and have shown aggression to shelter staff are unlikely adoptable. On the other hand, a dog may be submissive and overwhelmingly friendly, and it will go out for adoption right away. Often though there's a gray zone where an animal could go either way with temperament, and those cases are gut wrenching to decide. Shelter staff do not want to euthanize healthy animals, but they also want to protect the safety of community members who trust them to screen out dangerous animals. It's a quagmire without a good solution.

Not just dogs are evaluated for temperament, other animals such as hamsters, guinea pigs, birds, and cats are all also evaluated. I was surprised to discover at one shelter that almost all adult feral cats that had never been owned and were totally self-sufficient were euthanized. The shelter didn't have the resources to sterilize and release the cats, nor was it their policy to release unaltered animals back into the wild (as that would only contribute to more feral animals).

Neither open admission nor closed admission shelter system is without fault. "Kill" shelters are sometimes forced to euthanize healthy animals while "no kill" shelters can turn away any animal for any reason. As potential adopters, the best advice is to do your research and trust your judgment. It's important to know the differences between the types of shelters that exist to aid in any adoption decision.

11

Not All Shelter Animals Can or Will Be Adopted

Greg Allen

Greg Allen is a correspondent for National Public Radio. *Allen covers a wide range of topics and stories and is based in Florida.*

About two decades ago, San Francisco decided it was time to guarantee every adoptable dog and cat a home. It was a huge task to take on with the approximate 8 million animals across the US coming into shelters on a yearly basis. One problem with this goal is that not all animals taken into shelters are adoptable for some reason or another, and the question of how to deal with overcrowded shelters has become increasingly pressing. Of course, most shelter staff don't want to euthanize animals, but the issue of "no-kill" shelters has become problematic.

It's been 20 years since San Francisco helped start a revolution: It became the first US community to guarantee a home to every adoptable dog and cat.

Since then, the no-kill movement, as it's called, has been credited with greatly reducing the number of dogs and cats that are euthanized, from some 20 million down to about 3 million each year.

But like any movement, this one has had its disagreements— including what the term "no-kill" actually means. While some shelters indeed put no animals down, shelters are allowed to euthanize a percentage of their animals and still keep the no-kill designation. And some animal advocates say trying to place every animal in a home isn't advisable.

There are an estimated 14,000 shelters and pet rescue groups in the US, taking in nearly 8 million animals each year. Most are small groups, like Paws 4 You, founded 7 years ago in Miami by Carol Caridad. At any given time, she says, the shelter has between 80 and 95 dogs.

Paws 4 You works to find homes for dogs the group pulls from Miami-Dade Animal Services, the county-run shelter. And some dogs are easier to place than others. Caridad points out two, Charlene and Cisco, who have been with her for more than 3 years.

"They may react and get loud when they first see someone new," she says, "but they are all extremely loving."

If the dogs had not been taken from the county shelter, they likely would have been euthanized years ago.

Paws 4 You, like most pet rescue groups, operates a no-kill shelter. But the term means different things to different people. Caridad saves all her dogs—including one or two that aren't that friendly and may never be adopted.

But shelters can euthanize up to 10 percent of their animals for reasons of health and temperament, and still be considered "no-kill."

"The no-kill concept will be a constantly debated question among a lot of animal lovers, as to whether we are there or whether we are still working on getting to the goal," says Richard Avanzino, former head of San Francisco SPCA, which kick-started the no-kill movement in 1994.

Avanzino is now president of Maddie's Fund, a group that works to promote the no-kill movement. He says about 700,000 of the 3 million dogs killed each year are, as he calls it, "legitimate euthanizations"—animals that are unadoptable because of health or behavior.

But not all dog lovers embrace the no-kill philosophy. Patti Strand, director of the National Animal Interest Alliance, an organization that represents the American Kennel Club and other dog breeders, says "the word 'no-kill' has become, really, a marketing term."

Like just about all in the dog world, Strand supports shelters and adoptions. But she says the phrase no-kill is misleading. Unlike government-run, "open-access" shelters that take all the animals that come in, most no-kill shelters limit the number and types of dogs and cats they accept. For open-access shelters, Strand says the goal of adopting out 90 percent of the dogs taken in may not be practical—or safe.

Of particular concern, she says, are shelters in rural areas and the South, which take in large numbers of strays and unwanted dogs. "At some point, you begin to adopt out animals that have serious health issues or serious temperament issues that you should not," she says.

Strand says that in Portland, Ore., where she works with the American Kennel Club chapter, most of the calls to the group's help line come from people who have adopted dogs that turn out to have unexpected problems.

The no-kill movement has taken hold strongest in Northern states, from New England to the West Coast. In other states, like Florida, the supply of unwanted dogs still outstrips the demand—and euthanizations are still very much a fact of life.

In Miami, the county-run animal shelter takes in more than 15,000 dogs and 13,000 cats each year. In 2012, the county adopted a resolution that its shelter, the largest in Florida, would become a no-kill facility.

Alex Munoz, director of the Animal Services Department, says they're making progress toward that goal.

"Over the past few years we've increased our overall save rate from less than 50 percent to over 80 percent for both dogs and cats," he says.

But that still means Miami's animal shelter, while embracing the no-kill philosophy, euthanizes thousands of dogs and cats each year. It's a fact that upsets many rescue groups, some of whom have been critical of the county agency.

But Munoz says it all comes down to numbers. "The shelter is not an infinite space. There are 222 cages, and on any given day, there's more than 300 dogs."

Munoz says the agency is stepping up its spay and neuter program and holding more adoption events in the community, and hopes to get Miami close to the 90 percent no-kill goal within the next year.

12

Wild Animals Should Not Become Exotic Pets—It Is Risky and Dangerous

Born Free USA

Born Free USA is a nonprofit animal advocacy organization dedicated to keeping wild animals in the wild where they belong.

According to the authors of this viewpoint, wild animals should stay in their natural habitat and live out their lives there instead of being made to live as exotic pets. Despite this sounding like common sense, an incredibly large number of these creatures are captured in the wild, and then traded, sold, and forced to live miserable lives in captivity. Unfortunately, it is fairly easy to buy exotic animals, but it is difficult to provide proper care. Most wild animals cannot be effectively domesticated, and they pose various dangers to owners, the community where they live, and other people who come into contact with them.

E xotic animals—lions, tigers, wolves, bears, reptiles, non-human primates—belong in their natural habitat and not in the hands of private individuals as "pets." By their very nature, these animals are wild and potentially dangerous and, as such, do not adjust well to a captive environment.

Because the majority of states do not keep accurate records of exotic animals entering their state, it is impossible to determine exactly how many exotic animals are privately held as pets. The

"Get The Facts: The Dangers of Keeping Exotic 'Pets,'" Born Free USA. Reprinted by permission.

number is estimated to be quite high. An estimated 5,000 tigers alone are held by private individuals.

The American Veterinary Medical Association, the United States Department of Agriculture (USDA), and the Centers for Disease Control and Prevention (CDC) have all expressed opposition to the possession of certain exotic animals by individuals.

Exotic animals do not make good companions. They require special care, housing, diet, and maintenance that the average person cannot provide. When in the hands of private individuals the animals suffer due to poor care. They also pose safety and health risks to their possessors and any person coming into contact with them.

Individuals possessing exotic animals often attempt to change the nature of the animal rather than the nature of the care provided. Such tactics include confinement in small barren enclosures, chaining, beating "into submission," or even painful mutilations, such as declawing and tooth removal.

If and when the individual realizes he/she can no longer care for an exotic pet, he/she usually turns to zoos and other institutions such as sanctuaries to relieve him/her of the responsibility. However, all the zoos and accredited institutions could not possibly accommodate the number of unwanted exotic animals. Consequently, the majority of these animals are euthanized, abandoned, or doomed to live in deplorable conditions.

The Exotic Animal Pet Trade

Every year, a variety of sources provides millions of animals to the exotic pet trade. Animals are captured from their native habitat and transported to various countries to be sold as pets. Others are surplus animals from zoos or their offspring. Backyard breeders also supply exotic animals.

It is absurdly easy to obtain an exotic pet. More than 1000 Internet sites offer to sell, give care advice, and provide chat rooms where buyers and sellers can haggle over a price. Helping to facilitate the exotic pet trade is the *Animal Finders' Guide*, which carries ads from dealers, private parties, breeders, ranchers, and zoos offering large cats, monkeys, and other exotic animals for sale.

The sellers of these animals, however, make no mention of the state or local laws regulating private possession of exotics, or of the dangers, difficulties, physical and physiological needs of the animals they peddle. The suffering of the animals in the hands of unqualified and hapless buyers appears to be of no concern in the lucrative exotic pet trade.

Public Safety Risk

Exotic animals are inherently dangerous to the individuals who possess them, to their neighbors, and to the community at large. Across the country, many incidents have been reported where exotic animals held in private hands attacked humans and other animals, and escaped from their enclosure and freely roamed the community. Children and adults have been mauled by tigers, bitten by monkeys, and asphyxiated by snakes.

By their very nature, exotic animals are dangerous. Although most exotic animals are territorial and require group interactions, an exotic pet typically is isolated and spends the majority of his/her day in a small enclosure unable to roam and express natural behaviors freely. These animals are time bombs waiting to explode.

Monkeys are the most common non-human primates held by private individuals. At the age of two, monkeys begin to exhibit unpredictable behavior. Males tend to become aggressive, and both males and females bite to defend themselves and to establish dominance. Reported have been many monkey bites that resulted in serious injury to the individual who possessed the animal, to a neighbor, or to a stranger on the street. According to the CDC, 52 people reported being bitten by macaque monkeys between 1990 to 1997. CDC reported, however, that "owners of pet macaques are often reluctant to report bite injuries from their pets, even to their medical care providers" for fear that their animal will be confiscated and possibly killed.

Non-domesticated felines, such as lions, tigers, leopards, and cougars, are commonly held as pets. These exotic animals are cute and cuddly when they are young but have the potential to kill or seriously injure people and other animals as they grow. Even a seemingly friendly and loving animal can attack unsuspecting individuals. Many large cats have escaped from their cages and terrorized communities. Several of these incidents have resulted in either serious injury to the persons who came in contact with the animal, or the death of the animal, or both.

Reptiles, including all types of snakes and lizards, pose safety risks to humans as well. Many incidents have been reported of escapes, strangulations, and bites from pet reptiles across the country. Snakes are the most common "pet" reptiles—about 3% of US households possess 7.3 million pet reptiles—and have the potential to inflict serious injury through a bite or constriction. According to the University of Florida, more than 7,000 venomous snake bites are reported annually in the United States (it is uncertain how many of these snakes are pets), 15 of which result in death. Moreover, there have been several reported incidences involving strangulation by snakes. For example, on August 28, 1999, in Centralia, IL, a 3-year-old boy was strangled to death by the family's pet python. The parents were charged with child endangerment and unlawful possession of a dangerous animal.

Human Health Risk

Exotic animals pose serious health risks to humans. Many exotic animals are carriers of zoonotic diseases, such as Herpes B, Monkey Pox, and Salmonellosis, all of which are communicable to humans.

Herpes B-virus

80 to 90 percent of all macaque monkeys are infected with Herpes B-virus or Simian B, a virus that is harmless to monkeys but often fatal in humans. Monkeys shed the virus intermittently in saliva or genital secretions, which generally occurs when the monkey is ill, under stress, or during breeding season. At any given time, about

2% of infected macaque monkeys are shedding the virus. A person who is bitten, scratched, sneezed or spit on while shedding occurs runs the risk of contracting the disease. Monkeys rarely show any signs or symptoms of shedding, making it nearly impossible to know when one is at risk.

Reported cases of infection in humans are very rare; since the identification of the virus in 1932, there have only been 31 documented human infections by B virus, 21 of which were fatal. According to the CDC, the reason for "such an apparently low rate of transmission may include infrequent B virus shedding by macaques, cross-reactive immunity against B virus stimulated by herpes simplex virus infection, and undetected asymptomatic infection." However, the frequency of Herpes B infection in humans has never been adequately studied and thus it is difficult to quantify how many people are actually infected with the virus. Persons who possess or work with infected monkeys are presumed to be in constant peril of potentially contracting the virus.

Bites from non-human primates can cause severe lacerations. Wounds may become infected, with the potential to reach the bone and cause permanent deformity. The frequency of bites remains a mystery. Although it is widely acknowledged that non-human primate bites are some of the worst animal bites, little research regarding them exists.

Monkeys have also been known to transmit the Ebola virus, monkey pox, and other deadly illnesses.

Salmonellosis

Probably 90% of all reptiles carry and shed salmonella in their feces. Iguanas, snakes, lizards, and turtles are common carriers of the bacterium. Reptiles that carry salmonella do not show any symptoms, thus there is no simple way to tell which reptiles play host to the microbe and which do not, because even those that have it do not constantly shed the bacterium.

Salmonellosis associated with exotic pets has been described as one of the most important public health diseases affecting more people and animals than any other single disease. The CDC estimates that 93,000 salmonella cases caused by exposure to reptiles are reported each year in the United States.

Salmonella infection is caused when individuals eat after failing to wash their hands properly after handling a reptile or objects the reptile contaminated (this can be either indirect or direct contact with infected reptiles). Salmonella bacteria do not make the animal sick, but in people can cause serious cases of severe diarrhea (with or without blood), headache, malaise, nausea, fever, vomiting, abdominal cramps, and even death—especially in young children, the elderly, and those with immune-compromised systems. In addition, salmonella infection can result in sepsis and meningitis (particularly in children) as well as invade the intestinal mucosa and enter the bloodstream causing septicemia and death.

In March 1999, the CDC contacted every state health department to determine whether state regulations existed for sale of reptiles and distribution of information about contracting salmonella from reptiles. Forty-eight states responded—three (CA, CT, MI) had regulations requiring pet stores to provide information about salmonella to persons purchasing a turtle. Two states (KS, MD) require salmonella information to be provided to persons purchasing any reptile, and three states (AZ, MN, WY) prohibit reptiles in day care centers and long-term-care facilities.

During 1996–1998, 16 different state health departments reported to the CDC salmonella infections in persons who had direct or indirect contact with pet reptiles, and in 1994–1995, 13 different state health departments reported salmonella infections. The CDC recommends that children, people with compromised immune systems, and the elderly should avoid all contact with reptiles and not possess them as pets.

Laws Governing Private Possession of Exotic Animals

The sale and possession of exotic animals is regulated by a patchwork of federal, state and local laws that generally vary by community and by animal. Individuals possessing exotic animals must be in compliance with all federal laws as well as any state, city, and county laws.

Federal Laws

Three federal laws regulate exotic animals—the Endangered Species Act, the Public Health Service Act, and the Lacey Act. However, these laws primarily regulate the importation of exotic animals into the United States and not private possession.

Under the Endangered Species Act (ESA) it is illegal to possess, sell, or buy an endangered species regardless to whether it's over the Internet or not. The ESA does not regulate private possession, it merely allows the US Fish and Wildlife Service (USFWS) to prosecute individuals who illegally possess endangered species. It should be noted that "generic" tigers (subspecies that have been interbred) are not considered endangered and, as such, can be legally bred and possessed.

The Public Health Services Act prohibits the importation of non-human primates and their offspring into the United States after October 1975 for any use other than scientific, educational or exhibition purposes.

The Lacey Act allows the US government to prosecute persons in possession of an animal illegally obtained in a foreign country or another state. Again, this Act does not regulate private possession, it merely allows the USFWS to prosecute individuals who have illegally obtained exotic animals.

State Laws

The state governments possess the authority to regulate exotic animals privately held. Laws vary from state to state on the type of regulation imposed and the specific animals regulated. Thirteen states (AK, CA, CO, GA, HI, MA, NH, NJ, NM, TN, UT, VT,

WY) ban private possession of exotic animals (i.e. they prohibit possession of at least large cats, wolves, bears, non-human primates, and dangerous reptiles); seven states (CT, FL, IL, MD, MI, NE, VA) have a partial ban (i.e. they prohibit possession of some exotic animals but not all); fourteen states (AZ, DE, IN, ME, MS, MT, NY, ND, OK, OR, PA, RI, SD, TX) require a license or permit to possess exotic animals; and while the remaining states neither prohibit nor require a license, they may require some information from the possessor (veterinarian certificate, certification that animal was legally acquired, etc.).

Local Laws

Many cities and counties have adopted ordinances that are more stringent than the state law. Generally, the City or County Council have determined that possession of certain exotic species poses a serious threat to the health, safety, and welfare of the residents of the community as a result of a recent attack in the area, an escape, or by the virtue of the animals' physical attributes and natural behavior and, as such, adopts an ordinance regulating or banning private possession.

Some people often sidestep existing laws or bans by becoming licensed breeders or exhibitors under the USDA and/or by having their property rezoned. In addition, individuals often move out of city limits or to a new state once a restriction or ban is imposed.

What to Do

You can do several things to help stop private possession of exotic animals:

- For the animals' sake and for your health and safety, please do not buy exotic animals as "pets."
- If you observe an exotic animal being abused, living in deplorable conditions, etc., report it to the appropriate animal control agency.
- Educate others. Write a Letter to the Editor. Share this fact sheet with friends and family.

- Support legislation at all levels to prohibit private possession of exotic animals.
- Find out how your state, city and county regulates private possession of exotic animals. For more information, see our website. If your state, city or county does not prohibit private possession, contact your state senator and representative or your city and county council members and urge them to introduce legislation banning possession of exotic animals.

What Government Agencies and Public Officials Are Saying

- "The AVMA strongly opposes the keeping of wild carnivore species of animals [and reptiles and amphibians] as pets and believes that all commercial traffic of these animals for such purpose should be prohibited."—The American Veterinary Medical Association
- "Large wild and exotic cats such as lions, tigers, cougars, and leopards are dangerous animals … Because of these animals' potential to kill or severely injure both people and other animals, an untrained person should not keep them as pets. Doing so poses serious risks to family, friends, neighbors, and the general public. Even an animal that can be friendly and loving can be very dangerous."—The United States Department of Agriculture
- "Pet reptiles should be kept out of households where children aged less than 5 years or immunocompromised persons live. Families expecting a new child should remove the pet reptile from the home before the infant arrives."—The Centers for Disease Control and Prevention
- "Buying or giving exotic pets such as monkeys, hedgehogs, prairie dogs, reptiles, or other wildlife potentially can be dangerous to both humans and the animals themselves."—Veterinarian Jane Mahlow, Director of the Texas Department of Health Zoonosis Control Division

- "People buy these [large cats] when they're kittens and don't have the foresight to see in four years that kitten is going to be 500 pounds, and instead of two bottles it is going to need 30 to 50 pounds of meat a day. They try to make a pet out of something that will never be a pet."—Terry Mattive of T & D Mountain Range Menagerie, a sanctuary for unwanted, abused and exploited jungle cats in Penn Creek, PA
- "Macaques [monkeys] are aggressive and are known to carry diseases, including herpes B, which can be fatal to humans … My opinion is primates make very poor pets."—Dr. Michael Cranfield, veterinarian at the Baltimore Zoo and an expert on primates

13

The Exotic Pet Trade Depletes Wild Populations and Damages Ecosystems

Rob Laidlaw

Rob Laidlaw is a trained biologist and wildlife activist. He founded the international wildlife protection organization Zoocheck.

As this viewpoint shows, the worldwide trade in exotic pets is damaging to wild animal populations and their ecosystems. Unfortunately this trade is growing, and so too is the economic benefit for the people who partake in it. Not only are some pet species close to extinction, but escaped exotic pets also pose several different threats, including possibly spreading diseases to native species of wildlife or their human owners while in captivity. Various reptile species have grown in popularity as pets, but why, the viewpoint asks, should anyone seek exotic pets when there is an abundance of domesticated animals available as pets?

The craze for wild animals as pets has fuelled a worldwide trade that is now valued in the billions of dollars annually. Every day thousands of wild animals are in transit from one location to another. Captured from the wild by collectors in Asia, Africa, Latin America, Europe and North America, they are shipped by air to consumers around the world.

"The Exotic Pet Trade: Damaging, Wasteful and Cruel," Rob Laidlaw, Zoocheck, www. zoocheck.com. Reprinted by permission.

The global market for exotic pets has grown substantially in recent years. In the United States alone, 260 million live animals were imported in 2002. No one knows the exact extent of the trade in Canada because it is largely unregulated and untracked, but it is substantial.

Collection for the pet trade is now considered a major threat to wildlife around the world, depleting animal populations, driving species to extinction and disrupting ecosystems. In some areas of the world, entire habitats have been wiped clean of species that are popular in the pet trade. Even endangered and newly discovered species are sought after by pet trade collectors.

Wild animal pets also pose other kinds of threats. Throughout the world, privately-owned exotic pets escape or are abandoned to fend for themselves in the wild. Hundreds of species have now established themselves in foreign territories where they may compete with or displace native wildlife. For example, in Canada, red-eared slider turtles, who many experts believe aggressively compete with native turtles, have now established themselves in dozens of locations across the country.

Escaped or abandoned pets may also be carriers of new parasites and diseases that could have potentially devastating effects on native animals who have not evolved any natural defenses against them.

The wild animal pet trade also threatens human health and safety. New, potentially deadly zoonotic diseases that can be transmitted to humans are emerging with alarming frequency and many of them originate in wild animals. Throughout the world, public health agencies have recognized that the disease risks posed by the wild animal pet trade are serious and substantial.

In addition to the conservation concerns associated with the capture and trade of millions of wild animals, there can also severe welfare costs to each individual animal. The capture, transport and confinement of wild animals is an often brutal and cruel business, causing untold suffering and death.

The Reptile Pet Trade

Since the early 1990s, the reptile pet trade has grown by leaps and bounds. In fact, the trade has now reached a point where reptiles are considered a mainstay of the pet industry. While some reptiles are produced in captivity (the majority being red-eared sliders produced on turtle farms in the United States), the rest are still caught from the wild or are produced by wild-caught parents.

While large numbers of wild-caught reptiles come from Africa, Asia and Latin America, significant numbers are still being removed from the wild in other areas. The primary consumer markets for pet reptiles and other exotics are North America, Europe and Japan.

The explosion in popularity of reptiles as pets can be attributed to a number of different factors, such as the erroneous promotion of reptiles as easy to keep; an increase in the number and variety of imported reptiles; and an increase in the number of professional and amateur importers and reptile breeders.

An additional factor in the growth of the reptile trade is the emergence of restrictions on the trade in wild caught birds. Reduced availability of wild birds due to trade restrictions has caused suppliers to shift to alternate, exploitable species to fill the gap.

Unfortunately, the exact scale of the reptile pet trade remains a matter of guesswork. In many countries, reptiles are poorly tracked or not tracked at all, so information about the numbers they export is lacking. However, records from consumer countries clearly indicate that every year the trade involves many millions of individual reptiles representing at least 500–700 different species.

While the reptile pet trade in Canada has not been comprehensively studied, there is evidence to suggest that it has also experienced growth in recent years. A substantial number of reptiles are imported into Canada directly from their countries of origin, while others are re-exports from suppliers in the US. Imported reptiles come in all shapes and sizes and include both common and rare species.

Reptile Welfare

Unfortunately, reptiles are often subject to harsh handling and marginal conditions during the capture process. They may be trapped in nooses, nets and buckets or they may be chased and grabbed by hand.

Those that survive the capture process may be crammed into crude containers and shipped in the cargo holds of aircraft to destinations around the world. They may suffer from twisted tails and spines, broken limbs, torn claws or from being crushed by others that are stacked on top of them. Dehydrated and emaciated, many will die in transit. Some species, such as Florida softshell turtles and map turtles can suffer mortality rates as high as 30%.

If reptiles don't die in transit, they may die later from the long-term effects of capture and transport. Additional numbers may expire from the effects of inappropriate housing, poor husbandry and an inadequate diet provided by well-meaning but naive owners. Some experts estimate that 75%–90% of wild-caught reptiles don't survive beyond their first 12 months of captivity.

The wild animal pet trade is a largely wasteful and unnecessary industry. Species are being driven to extinction, ecosystems are being disrupted and millions of individual animals are forced to suffer. Reptiles kept as pets also pose significant risks to human health and safety through the transmission of zoonotic diseases. They also pose a disease threat to native wildlife populations when they escape or are abandoned to fend for themselves. A wide variety of domesticated animal species are currently available as pets, so there is little justification for continuation of the wild animal pet trade. For these reasons, Zoocheck recommends that members of the public refrain from purchasing or keeping wild animals, including reptiles, as pets.

14

Effective Strategies to Combat the Wildlife Trade

The White House

The Obama administration actively worked to protect wildlife by combatting the wildlife trade. Wildlife preservation continues to be a goal of the US government.

The exotic pet trade encourages wildlife trafficking and is a threat to animals, people, and the government. When in office, President Obama sought to decrease this illicit trade, a market that, unfortunately, is heavily influenced by both legal and illegal demand for animals in the US. Asian markets also demand various animals and wildlife products, and dealers in Africa have stepped in to meet this demand to the detriment of wild animals. The US implemented a plan to strengthen laws and regulations that affect wildlife and ecosystems within the continental borders of the United States, and continued to extend advocacy efforts to protect wildlife outside the US.

In the past decade, wildlife trafficking—the poaching or other taking of protected or managed species and the illegal trade in wildlife and their related parts and products—has escalated into an international crisis. Wildlife trafficking is both a critical conservation concern and a threat to global security with

"National Strategy for Combating Wildlife Trafficking," The White House, February 11, 2014. https://obamawhitehouse.archives.gov/sites/default/files/docs/ nationalstrategywildlifetrafficking.pdf. Licensed under CC BY 3.0 US.

significant effects on the national interests of the United States and the interests of our partners around the world.

As President Obama said in Tanzania in July 2013, on issuing a new Executive Order to better organize United States Government efforts in the fight against wildlife trafficking, wildlife is inseparable from the identity and prosperity of the world as we know it. We need to act now to reverse the effects of wildlife trafficking on animal populations before we lose the opportunity to prevent the extinction of iconic animals like elephants and rhinoceroses. Like other forms of illicit trade, wildlife trafficking undermines security across nations. Well-armed networks of poachers, criminals, and corrupt officials exploit porous borders and weak institutions to profit from trading in illegally taken wildlife.

We know that the United States is among the world's major markets for wildlife and wildlife products, both legal and illegal. In Asia, increased demand for ivory and rhino horn stems from a rapidly expanding wealthy class that views these commodities as luxury goods that enhance social status. As a result, we have seen an increase in ready buyers within Africa who serve as dealers to clients in Asia. Increased demand for elephant ivory and rhino horn has triggered dramatic and rapid upticks in poaching in Africa. Criminal elements of all kinds, including some terrorist entities and rogue security personnel—often in collusion with government officials in source countries—are involved in poaching and transporting ivory and rhino horn across Africa. We assess with high confidence that traffickers use sophisticated networks and take advantage of jurisdictions where public officials are complicit in order to move elephant ivory and rhino horn from remote areas to markets and ports, perpetuating corruption and border insecurity, particularly in key eastern, central, and southern African states. Some of these networks are likely the same or overlap with those that also deal in other illicit goods such as drugs and weapons.

Poaching presents significant security challenges for militaries and police forces in African nations, which are often outgunned by poachers and their criminal and extremist allies. Moreover, wildlife trafficking corrodes democratic institutions and undermines transparency. Corruption and lack of sufficient penal and financial deterrents are hampering these governments' abilities to reduce poaching and trafficking. Material and training, legal, and diplomatic support could have a significant impact on the trajectory of the illicit rhino horn and ivory trades, and would also represent a relatively cost-effective way to gain new insights into the behavior of implicated criminal groups and associated trafficking networks. However, the widespread complicity of military and government officials in the trade hinders potential partnerships.

Why Now?

The scale and scope of wildlife trafficking continue to grow at an alarming rate, reversing decades of conservation gains. Wildlife trafficking threatens an increasing variety of terrestrial, freshwater, and marine species, including but not limited to: elephants, rhinos, tigers, sharks, tuna, sea turtles, land tortoises, great apes, exotic birds, pangolins, sturgeon, coral, iguanas, chameleons, and tarantulas. Wildlife trafficking is facilitated and exacerbated by illegal harvest and trade in plants and trees, which destroys needed habitat and opens access to previously remote populations of highly endangered wildlife, such as tigers. In addition, illegal trafficking of fisheries products, among others, threatens food supplies and food security. Many species decimated by illegal trade and other threats, such as habitat loss, are now in danger of extinction. Wildlife trafficking jeopardizes the survival of iconic species such as elephants and rhinos. Now is the time for greater action, before such losses become irreversible.

The United States has long placed great value and importance on conserving wildlife resources within and beyond our borders. Federal law has protected some of this Nation's species from poaching and illegal commercialization for more than a century. As the first Nation to ratify the Convention on International Trade in Endangered Species of Wild Fauna and Flora (CITES) in 1974, the United States has consistently stood with countries around the world in combating wildlife trafficking and protecting natural resources.

Conservation efforts to protect biodiversity and preserve functioning ecosystems are critical to secure economic prosperity, regional stability, and human health around the world. Wildlife trafficking now threatens not only national and global wildlife resources but also national and global security. This reality requires that we strengthen our efforts at home and abroad and ensure that the agencies tasked with this work have adequate resources, appropriate authorities, and the necessary partnerships to do it well.

This strategy sets forth a broad and time-sensitive course of action. This crisis must be addressed aggressively and quickly, or it will be too late.

US Strategic Priorities

We have identified three strategic priorities to respond to the global wildlife trafficking crisis and address related threats to US national interests:

1. Strengthen enforcement;
2. Reduce demand for illegally traded wildlife; and
3. Build international cooperation, commitment, and public-private partnerships.

To meet these strategic goals, we will expand United States Government leadership guided by the following principles.

- Marshal Federal Resources for Combating Wildlife Trafficking by elevating this issue as a core missions of all relevant executive branch agencies and departments and ensuring effective coordination across our government.
- Use Resources Strategically by identifying common priorities and strategic approaches and by coordinating and harmonizing

funding and programs across agencies to maximize strategic impact and minimize duplication of efforts.

- Improve the Quality of Available Information by developing and using innovative and science-based tools to gather and appropriately share the information needed to fight wildlife trafficking and to assess and improve our and our partners' efforts.
- Consider All Links of the Illegal Trade Chain in developing and evaluating strategies to establish strong and effective long-term solutions that address all aspects of wildlife trafficking, from poaching and transit through consumer use.
- Strengthen Relationships and Partnerships with the many public and private partners who share our commitment and our belief that continued coordination among nations, as well as with nongovernmental organizations and the private sector, are key to stopping wildlife trafficking.

Strengthen Enforcement

To fight wildlife trafficking, all countries must have the investigative, enforcement, and judicial capabilities to respond to these crimes and disrupt wildlife trafficking networks.

US Domestic Enforcement

Wildlife trafficking occurs across and within our borders. The United States is among the world's major markets for wildlife and wildlife products, both legal and illegal. Our country also serves as a transit point for trafficked wildlife moving from range (or source) countries to other markets around the globe and as a source for illegally taken wildlife entering the global trade. We will treat wildlife trafficking as the serious crime it is and work to ensure that our enforcement efforts adequately protect wildlife resources. To accomplish this goal, the United States Government will:

- Assess and Strengthen Legal Authorities—We will analyze and assess the laws, regulations, and enforcement tools that the United States can use against wildlife trafficking to determine which are most effective and which need strengthening to better deter wildlife trafficking and foster successful investigation and prosecution of wildlife traffickers. We will work with the Congress to seek legislation that recognizes wildlife trafficking crimes as predicate offenses for money laundering, thus placing wildlife trafficking on an equal footing with other serious crimes.

- Use Administrative Tools to Quickly Address Current Poaching Crisis—We propose to immediately pursue a series of administrative actions to establish a US ban with limited exceptions on elephant ivory and rhino horn trade in response to unparalleled and escalating threats to these species. We will strengthen controls on the commercial import of African elephant ivory by eliminating broad administrative exceptions to the 1989 African Elephant Conservation Act moratorium. We will ensure that African elephants receive the same protections as other threatened or endangered species by revoking the regulatory exemption that allows African elephant ivory to be traded in ways that would otherwise be prohibited by the Endangered Species Act. We will limit the number of elephant sport-hunting trophies that an individual can import, adopting the same rule that now exists for leopard trophies. We will improve the protections that the Endangered Species Act provides for all species listed as threatened or endangered by clarifying the regulations that implement the statute's exemptions for commercial trade of 100-year old antiques. We will also improve our ability to protect elephants, rhinos, and other CITES-listed wildlife by finalizing a proposed rule that will reaffirm and improve public understanding of the "use after import" provisions in U.S. CITES regulations, which strictly limit sales, including intrastate sales, of wildlife that was imported for noncommercial purposes.

- Strengthen Interdiction and Investigative Efforts—We will enhance efforts to curb the illegal flow of wildlife products across and within US borders. We will strengthen Federal wildlife import/export regulations as needed and optimize the wildlife inspection presence at US ports of entry. We will target wildlife trafficking and distribution networks within the United States by conducting criminal investigations, identifying weak international trade controls, and disrupting illicit finance tied to wildlife traffickers. We will pursue prosecutions in the United States to remove key leaders and operatives and to break up syndicates.
- Prioritize Wildlife Trafficking Across U.S. Enforcement Agencies—We will work to improve interagency cooperation to detect, interdict, and investigate wildlife trafficking. We will assess ways to augment the law enforcement capacities of the US Fish and Wildlife Service and the National Oceanic and Atmospheric Administration with other law enforcement agencies. Recognizing that state and tribal law protects many key species that are subject to illegal exploitation, we will strengthen and sustain Federal partnerships with states, local and territorial governments, and tribes to protect domestic resources from poaching and illegal trade.
- Enhance Coordination Among and Between Enforcement and Intelligence Agencies—We will assess ways to increase coordination among law enforcement and intelligence agencies to enhance the effectiveness of Federal efforts to combat wildlife trafficking. For example, we will seek to establish and institutionalize appropriate pathways for conveying intelligence gathered on transnational organizations involved in wildlife trafficking to the enforcement agencies charged with investigating such crimes.
- Take the Profit Out of Wildlife Trafficking—We must target the assets of wildlife trafficking networks to make wildlife trafficking less profitable. We will seize the financial gains of wildlife traffickers in prosecutions, using all appropriate tools:

fines and penalties, both criminal and civil, forfeiture of assets and instrumentalities, and restitution for those victimized by wildlife crimes. Where possible, we will ensure that funds generated through prosecutions are directed back to conservation efforts or to combating wildlife trafficking. We will work with the Congress to provide language to allow for investing funds generated through wildlife trafficking prosecutions into conservation efforts or to combating wildlife trafficking, as well as to ensure adequate authority to forfeit all proceeds of wildlife trafficking and to assess whether current fine and penalty provisions provide adequate deterrence.

Global Enforcement

We will continue to help range, transit, and consumer countries identify gaps and build capacity for investigating and prosecuting wildlife trafficking. We will also continue to work directly with other countries to pursue and to provide operational support for multinational wildlife trafficking enforcement operations. To accomplish this goal, the United States Government will:

- Support Governments in Building Capacity—We will continue to collaborate with foreign government partners in building their capacity to stop poaching and illegal wildlife trade and to develop and effectively enforce wildlife trafficking laws. These efforts will focus on building the capacity to fight wildlife trafficking at all critical stages of enforcement: crafting strong laws, stopping poachers, protecting borders, investigating traffickers, fighting trafficking-related corruption, improving professionalism, strengthening judicial and prosecutorial effectiveness, building and bringing strong cases, and obtaining penalties adequate to deter others.
- Support Community-Based Wildlife Conservation—We will support efforts to work with local communities to protect wildlife and prevent wildlife trafficking. Local communities are essential partners on the ground and can be a powerful force in

support of wildlife conservation and a frontline defense against poaching. We will support efforts to help create alternative livelihoods to poaching (when applicable) and encourage local community members to participate directly in wildlife protection activities, including intelligence networks and developing channels for the public to report crimes.

- Support Development and Use of Effective Technologies and Analytical Tools—We will emphasize the importance of developing and disseminating cost-effective and accurate tools to support wildlife trafficking investigations and prosecutions, including technology that can be used to develop admissible evidence on species' identity and the geographic origin of wildlife parts and products. We will support analytic tools and technological solutions that can assist with identifying poaching hotspots or addressing the wildlife trafficking supply chain. We will also seek to further develop law enforcement tools and techniques to address cyber activities related to the selling and purchasing of illegal wildlife products on the Internet.
- Enhance Information Sharing—We will seek to ensure that intelligence activities are appropriately integrated in our international enforcement efforts. We will share information, as appropriate, on transnational criminal organizations, terrorist entities and rogue security personnel and the corrupt officials, individuals, and entities that facilitate these enterprises. Consistent with established priorities and resources, we will focus on financial networks linking source, transit, and demand countries, particularly those networks that pose the greatest threat to US national security interests. We will also work with our partner countries by helping them build their capacity to collect and analyze information, particularly for intelligence, forensic, investigative, and prosecutorial purposes.
- Participate in Multinational Enforcement Operations— We will build on the enforcement success that the United States has had in working with the international community

by increasing the advice and assistance we provide for multinational wildlife trafficking enforcement operations and by supporting and engaging in joint operations with enforcement authorities of other nations or multinational and intergovernmental bodies.

- Seek to Develop an Effective Worldwide Wildlife Enforcement Networks (WENS)—We will continue to support regional WENs and encourage greater cooperation between the WENs that are already operating in a number of regions. We will support the development of additional regional WENs where appropriate, with the ultimate objective of developing a strong and effective worldwide network of WENs.

- Address Wildlife Trafficking in Fighting Other Transnational Organized Crime—We will increase coordination among the agencies that lead our efforts to combat wildlife trafficking and those that lead our efforts to stop transnational organized crime so that wildlife trafficking issues are addressed, as appropriate, through the implementation of the *Strategy to Combat Transnational Organized Crime* (July 19, 2011).

- Focus on Corruption and Illicit Financial Flows—We will increase our efforts with our partner countries to target the corrupt public officials who make wildlife trafficking possible by linking technical assistance with anticorruption cooperation and efforts. We will coordinate with international partners to target the assets and impede the financial efforts of wildlife traffickers. We will also work to identify corrupt foreign officials, entities, or individuals who work with wildlife traffickers, and target their assets for forfeiture and repatriation to affected governments as appropriate.

Reduce Demand for Illegally Traded Wildlife

Increasing antipoaching and antitrafficking enforcement efforts will have only limited effect unless we work simultaneously to address the persistent market demand that drives this trade.

Criminals will continue to kill wildlife and traffic in contraband as long as the potential profits outweigh the risks. We must enlist individual consumers in our country and other nations in this fight by educating them about the impacts of wildlife trafficking, on people as well as wildlife, and encouraging them to examine their purchasing patterns in a context broader than personal desire or cultural tradition. At the same time, we recognize that markets for illegally traded wildlife exist for different reasons around the world and that approaches that work well in the United States may find less success elsewhere. To accomplish this goal, the United States Government will:

- Raise Public Awareness and Change Behavior—We will work to raise public awareness and recognition of wildlife trafficking and its negative impacts on species, the environment, security, food supplies, the economy, and human health. We will work with public and private partners to communicate the details and hard truths about these activities. By reproposing the retailing of the Save Vanishing Species Semi-Postal Stamp, we can provide the public an avenue to participate in financing antitrafficking efforts. It is not enough to increase public awareness; we will also target consumption patterns and look for opportunities to promote public engagement more directly. Applying the lessons learned from past campaigns, we will craft our messages and structure our efforts with the assistance of those with expertise and experience in developing, implementing, evaluating, and refining effective public communication strategies and educational tools.
- Build Partnerships to Reduce Domestic Demand—We will work with partners across the United States, including nongovernmental organizations and diaspora communities, to reduce domestic demand for illegally traded wildlife and wildlife products. We must team more effectively with the transportation industry, the tourism sector, restaurant and

hotel associations, those in the exotic pet industry, companies operating internet marketplaces, and other private sector entities in this effort. We will strengthen our partnerships with nongovernmental organizations, civil society groups, private donors, the media, and academia that focus on research and building political will to stop wildlife trafficking and combat the organized criminal networks that conduct or facilitate it.

- Promote Demand Reduction Efforts Globally—We will encourage, support, and collaborate with all other interested governments to launch public information campaigns to discourage the sale and purchase of illegally traded wildlife. We will implement a public diplomacy strategy that uses local voices and partners with communities and international nongovernmental organizations to reduce the demand for illegally traded wildlife products in key markets. We will respect cultural and national sensitivities even as we ask communities to reconsider longstanding traditions that might incentivize or contribute to wildlife trafficking.

Build International Cooperation, Commitment, and Public-Private Partnerships

Combating wildlife trafficking requires the engagement of governments in source, transit, and consumer countries throughout the world. We look to promote commitments to conservation and wildlife crime-fighting not only within countries that face this challenge but to facilitate cooperation across borders, among regions, and globally. We recognize that our efforts to engage the world in addressing wildlife trafficking must reach beyond governments and must recruit, embrace, and empower partners old and new—partners that range from nonprofit conservation groups to grass-roots activists, and from industries related to both legal and illegal wildlife trade to the media who report on them. And effective change requires political support, commitment and participation at all levels. To accomplish this goal, the United States Government will:

- Use Diplomacy to Catalyze Political Will—We will actively build on our successful efforts in the G-8, Asia-Pacific Economic Cooperation (APEC), and the UN Crime Commission to secure commitments from governments to take action and to treat wildlife trafficking as a serious crime. We will seek to work through other international fora, including the G-20, the Organization of American States, and the Organization for Economic Cooperation and Development, and the African Union, its subsidiaries, and African subregional bodies, to focus on wildlife trafficking and further strengthen international cooperation. We will continue to build support through regional and bilateral efforts, such as the bilateral dialogue on wildlife trafficking we launched as part of the United States-China Strategic and Economic Dialogue in July 2013.
- Strengthen International Arrangements that Protect Wildlife—We will expand our role to strengthen and ensure effective implementation of international agreements and other arrangements, particularly CITES, the principal international agreement that specifically addresses unsustainable and illegal wildlife, timber, and plant trade. We will work with the CITES Secretariat and other parties to adopt appropriate measures in response to accelerated or new threats and to improve global implementation of, and compliance with, the Treaty's requirements. We will support regional fishery management organizations to better detect and suppress Illegal, Unreported, and Unregulated (IUU) fishing and work with other international organizations to improve compliance and enforcement to protect wildlife and the habitats upon which wildlife depends.
- Use Existing and Future Trade Agreements and Initiatives to Protect Wildlife—We will engage trading partner countries

on a regional and bilateral basis under existing and future US free trade agreements, environmental cooperation mechanisms, and other trade-related initiatives to take measures to combat wildlife trafficking and to integrate wildlife trafficking and resource protection as priority areas for information exchange, cooperation, and capacity building.

- Incorporate Provisions to Protect Wildlife in Other International Agreements—We will seek opportunities to ensure wildlife trafficking is appropriately covered under relevant international agreements. We will seek provisions that ensure wildlife trafficking and related offenses are extraditable offenses under extradition treaties where appropriate. We will also seek to ensure wildlife trafficking and related offenses are covered in mutual legal assistance treaties, including with respect to assistance in freezing and seizing the illicit proceeds of wildlife trafficking, where appropriate.

- Cooperate with Other Governments—We will cooperate with and assist wildlife range countries to strengthen their capacity to tackle poachers and wildlife traffickers by providing technical assistance, training, and support, as well as by facilitating information sharing. We will help to secure key wildlife populations and habitats; provide information on the status of targeted species and of groups involved in poaching and trafficking; help to enhance governance for the conservation and sustainable use of wildlife and other natural resources; and leverage wildlife trafficking with efforts in other areas, such as conservation of forest habitat, to develop synergies. We will engage key transit countries and encourage them to control goods passing through their territory. We will also seek to work with like-minded consumer countries in these efforts as well, as in efforts to reduce demand.

- Promote Effective Partnerships—We will promote joint efforts by governments, intergovernmental organizations, the private sector, nongovernmental organizations, media, academia, and individuals to address wildlife trafficking. We will work on the ground with and through local communities and conservation groups to develop and sustain antipoaching efforts, stimulate alternative livelihoods, and create support for community-based economically-viable wildlife conservation and antipoaching efforts. We will continue to support and coordinate with international groups and coalitions that target wildlife trafficking and will invite other governments and organizations to join us to take collective action, leverage resources, maximize impact, and minimize duplication of efforts. We will build partnerships with the private sector to share and implement best practices that will support sustainable supply chains and avoid contribution to illegal wildlife trade. We will also work with partners in industries, including those that deal with live wildlife or use legally traded wildlife, to promote mechanisms that reduce the risk of illegal products entering the supply chain and assure consumers that the products they purchase were obtained legally and sustainably.

- Encourage Development of Innovative Approaches—We will leverage the United States technological expertise and our convening power to promote creative ideas, innovative solutions, and strategic partnerships to address forensic, financial, and other key issues to increase our sophistication ahead of the criminals involved in this illegal trade chain. We will challenge the private sector, the nongovernmental organizations and academic communities, and partner countries to think beyond business as usual.

Conclusion

This *Strategy* recognizes that we must redouble our efforts to address wildlife trafficking now if we are to preserve species and promote global peace and economic stability. The actions needed to disrupt and deter wildlife trafficking are clear, as are the consequences of failing to act both quickly and strategically in response to this multidimensional threat. The United States must curtail its own role in the illegal trade in wildlife and must lead in addressing this issue on the global stage. By working across Federal departments and agencies, the Presidential Task Force on Wildlife Trafficking, in consultation with the Advisory Council, will implement this strategy and collaborate where appropriate with the nongovernmental organizations and the private sector to ensure success. We can strengthen and expand enforcement and demand reduction efforts and promote and secure global commitment and cooperation in combating wildlife trafficking. In all of our endeavors, we must foster and strengthen partnerships with other governments, the nonprofit conservation community, and the private sector. No one country can tackle these issues on its own. This is a global challenge that requires global solutions. It is only by working together that we can develop effective solutions to combat wildlife trafficking and protect our natural resources for future generations.

15

Wild Animals Should Be Wild, Not Forced to Be Pets

The Humane Society of the United States

The Humane Society of the United States is an organization dedicated to animal protection.

People who sell wild animals as pets often mislead buyers into thinking that it is possible to appropriately care for wild animals, and that they will be domesticated like a dog or cat. In fact, it is nearly impossible to domesticate these creatures. Wild animals may be cute when they're young, but they grow up to be an instinctively wild creature meant for life in its natural habitat, not the life in captivity found in a private home or animal sanctuary.

The Humane Society of the United States strongly opposes keeping wild animals as pets. This principle applies to both native and nonnative species, whether caught in the wild or bred in captivity. The overwhelming majority of people who obtain these animals are unable to provide the care they require.

Caring for Wild Animals Is Difficult or Impossible

Despite what animal sellers may say, appropriate care for wild animals requires considerable expertise, specialized facilities, and lifelong dedication to the animals. Their nutritional and social needs are demanding to meet and, in many cases, are unknown.

"Should Wild Animals Be Kept as Pets?" The Humane Society of the United States. Reprinted by permission.

They often grow to be larger, stronger, and more dangerous than owners expect or can manage. Even small monkeys and small cats such as ocelots can inflict serious injuries, especially on children. Wild animals also pose a danger to human health and safety through disease and parasites.

Baby Animals Grow Up

Baby animals can be irresistibly adorable—until the cuddly baby becomes bigger and stronger than the owner ever imagined. The instinctive behavior of the adult animal replaces the dependent behavior of the juvenile, resulting in biting, scratching, or displaying destructive behaviors without provocation or warning. Such animals typically become too difficult to manage and are confined to small cages, passed from owner to owner, or disposed of in other ways. There are not enough reputable sanctuaries or other facilities to properly care for unwanted wild animals. They can end up back in the exotic pet trade. Some may be released into the wild where, if they survive, they can disrupt the local ecosystem.

Wild Animals Spread Disease

The Centers for Disease Control and Prevention discourages direct contact with wild animals for a simple reason: They can carry diseases that are dangerous to people, such as rabies, herpes B virus, and Salmonella. The herpes B virus commonly found among macaque monkeys can be fatal to humans. Tens of thousands of people get Salmonella infections each year from reptiles or amphibians, causing the CDC to recommend that these animals be kept out of homes with children under five. A 2003 outbreak of monkeypox was set in motion when African rodents carrying the disease were imported for the pet trade and infected native prairie dogs, who were also sold as pets.

Domestication Takes Centuries

Wild animals are not domesticated simply by being captive born or hand-raised. It's a different story with dogs and cats, who have been domesticated by selective breeding for desired traits over thousands of years. These special animal companions depend on humans for food, shelter, veterinary care, and affection. Wild animals, by nature, are self-sufficient and fare best without our interference. The instinctive behavior of these animals makes them unsuitable as pets.

Capturing Wild Animals Threatens Their Survival

The global wildlife trade threatens the very existence of some species in their native habitats. When wild-caught animals are kept as pets, their suffering may begin with capture—every year countless birds and reptiles suffer and die on the journey to the pet store. Animals meant to live in the wild may languish in a cramped backyard cage or circle endlessly in a cat carrier or aquarium. Often, they become sick or die because their owners are unable to care for them properly. Captive breeding is no solution. It does not take the wild out of wildlife.

Having any animal as a pet means being responsible for providing appropriate and humane care. Where wild animals are concerned, meeting this responsibility is usually impossible. People, animals, and the environment suffer the consequences.

16

Contact with Animals Can Also Harm Humans

Claire Asher

Claire Asher is a science writer and communicator with a PhD in genetics, ecology, and evolution from the University of Leeds and the Institute of Zoology. In addition to writing, she works as an innovation officer for the London NERC Doctoral Training Partnership at University College London.

While concerns about animals and their well being are certainly worth consideration, one should also keep in mind the potential health impacts that interacting with animals can have on humans. In fact, there are a number of zoonotic diseases, meaning diseases that can be transmitted from animals to humans. Common causes of zoonotic diseases include working with livestock, working as a veterinarian, hunting, and eating wild game. Furthermore, the prevalence of zoonotic diseases has increased over time and shows no sign of slowing down unless we become more conscientious in our interactions with animals.

In 1998, pig farmers in Malaysia suddenly started falling ill and doctors didn't know why. Within days of their first symptoms— headaches and fever—many of the farmers were hospitalized as their brains swelled. They suffered seizures or fell into comas. About half of those infected died.

More and more new cases appeared, but nobody knew where they were coming from. The Malaysian government blamed the disease on mosquitoes, telling people that everything was under control because they were spraying insecticide. But then one persistent researcher, Dr. Kaw Bing Chua, tested some samples at the Centers for Disease Control and Prevention in Colorado.

Chua found that the disease—which had been named Nipah after the town it emerged in—was a new member of a family called "paramyxoviridae," which also includes measles. These viruses come from livestock, not mosquitoes, and often infect the lungs— so they can spread through the air. He immediately phoned the Malaysian government and told them the news.

The government listened—and organized the country's largest ever animal culling program. More than a million pigs were herded into pits and shot. In the months that followed, nearly 300 people fell ill with Nipah; around 40 percent of cases were fatal and another 20 percent of patients suffered long-term neurological effects. But by June the following year the outbreak was over: Nipah had been successfully contained.

Nipah virus was a classic example of a "zoonosis": a disease being transmitted from animals to humans, or vice versa. Zoonotic disease includes many of our most formidable foes: Ebola, malaria, bird flu, and severe acute respiratory syndrome (SARS), to name just a few.

Another common example is food poisoning, which is often caused by bacteria in the genus *Campylobacter*. The bacterium usually infects poultry, but the birds display no clinical symptoms. Basic food hygiene practices and thorough cooking are enough to kill the bacterium, but still one in ten people fall ill with a *Campylobacter* infection each year.

There are relatively few examples of communicable diseases with absolutely no history of zoonosis, but Poliovirus—which causes the debilitating disease polio in about one in four of people infected with it—is one pathogen that is truly unique to humans.

Zoonotic diseases can be transmitted any time there is contact between humans and wildlife. Tending livestock, veterinary work, hunting, and eating wild animals are all common causes. Zoonotic pathogens can be bacterial, viral, or fungal, and DNA evidence suggest that they represent a startling 70 percent of all human diseases.

But a pathogen is not necessarily harmful to all animals it infects. Many species are able to act as "reservoir hosts"—carrying the infection but displaying no symptoms. This can make it difficult to spot new zoonotic diseases before they spread.

Bats, in particular, have been found to harbor a disproportionate number of emerging zoonoses. SARS, Ebola and even some Nipah outbreaks have been linked to human contact with a type of fruit bat called flying foxes. We don't know precisely what makes bats so ideally suited to act as reservoir hosts, but their relatively long lifespan, tendency to live in groups, and ability to fly long distances all help. Fruit-eating bats are also extremely common, occurring pretty much everywhere in the world that there is fruit.

Adapting to the immune defenses of a new host species is no mean feat for any pathogen. To most microorganisms, our bodies are as inhospitable as the Moon. The vast majority of diseases in other animals are likely to stay there.

Sometimes a single strain of a zoonotic disease will evolve to infect many different host species. In other cases, adapting to a new host results in an entirely new strain, specific to the new host species. Take human immunodeficiency virus (HIV), for example—new HIV-1 and HIV-2 strains are thought to have evolved from simian immunodeficiency viruses (SIVs) in the first half of the 20th century.

But even after a jump from humans to animals has occurred, the path to a pandemic is not straightforward—HIV-1 M didn't to reach pandemic levels for another six decades, when growing urban populations and increased promiscuity created the perfect conditions for the disease to spread. Since 1981 this strain has infected 60 million people and caused at least 25 million deaths.

Although animal diseases have probably always infected humans, increased urbanization and international travel have facilitated a boom in zoonoses. Between 1940 and 2004, animal-borne infections represented 60 percent of all emerging infectious diseases. China, which researchers believe to have been the origin of the Black Death in the 1300s, has been described as a "cradle of zoonosis" in modern times, because of its combined profile of rapid urbanization, globalization, and income growth. It was the birthplace of H5N1 avian influenza in the 1990s and SARS in the 2000s.

China isn't the only source of zoonoses. The recent Ebola pandemic caused devastation across Africa and panic around the world. Like HIV, Ebola is not a new disease—it has existed at relatively low levels since the 1970s. Small outbreaks periodically erupted in humans and wildlife, but it wasn't until 2013 that the disease reached pandemic levels, killing over 11,000 people worldwide.

Research interest in zoonotic diseases has spiked in recent decades, but even accounting for this extra effort, the number of emerging infectious diseases has increased steadily since 1940, with the majority originating in animals. This seems to be linked to a growing human population that is wealthier, travels more, and is living in increasingly dense urban areas, offering plenty of opportunities for diseases to spread.

An analysis of zoonotic diseases affecting over 2,800 species of mammal found that zoonoses are more likely to spill over into humans from species whose range overlaps with either those of other mammals, or with urban environments. The viruses most likely to make the jump to humans were those that already infect many species, are transmitted by arthropods such as mosquitoes and ticks, and those that possess certain cellular traits.

Climate change is also lending a helping hand. In 2016, researchers led by Kate Jones and David Redding at University College London developed a computer model to predict future outbreaks of Lassa fever in Africa. Lassa, which currently infects up to a million people a year in sub-Saharan Africa, causes a hemorrhagic fever that can be fatal.

The model predicted that cases of Lassa will double by 2070. The increase will largely be driven by climate change, which will expand the suitable habitat for the species of rat that spreads the disease, along with growing human populations and urbanization. The team said that their model could also be applied to predicting future outbreaks of Ebola and Zika virus.

We can't stop diseases from making the jump from animals to humans. But by predicting which diseases represent the highest risk, we can take steps to reduce contact with host animals, vaccinate humans and animals against infection, and monitor new outbreaks to prevent them developing into pandemics.

Databases tracking human outbreaks of known pathogens can offer an early-warning system for pandemics, and some novel surveillance systems have recently been developed to monitor the levels of disease in wild animal populations. One new technique uses blood-sucking flies as flying syringes, collecting samples of blood from wildlife that can later be tested for zoonotic diseases by scientists.

Vaccination can also defend us against known zoonotic diseases, but research and development efforts tend to be skewed towards pathogens affecting the developed world, missing major hotspots of zoonoses in developing regions. And while vaccination programs may be effective for livestock, they are more challenging to administer to wild animals.

Those wild animals present a limitless pool of potential new diseases that could threaten humans. Targeted monitoring and containment, combined with preventative measures such as education programs to reduce bush hunting, or improved farm designs that minimize contact between livestock and wild animals, may be our best hope to minimize the risk of pandemic.

As the 1999 Nipah virus outbreak came to an end, both Malaysians and virologists breathed a sigh of relief. But further outbreaks followed in Bangladesh and India in 2001, where they have since become a regular event, reminding us that while the battle may have been won, the war has not. Many researchers are now concerned that new strains of the virus might emerge in Africa, where contact with potential hosts such as bats and pigs is common.

Nipah can be contracted from bodily fluids of infected animals, and pigs are thought to catch the disease by eating fruit contaminated by infected bats or contact with bat droppings. Monitoring Nipah virus in livestock, as well as minimizing contact between humans and pigs, will be important measures to prevent a repeat jump of Nipah into humans from happening.

Currently Nipah virus can only be contracted by humans coming into contact with infected animals, although direct transmission from human to human has now been reported in a few cases. Since no antiviral treatment has been developed for the disease, the only way to slow an outbreak is to cull and carefully dispose of infected animals. There is no cure.

But it may be only a matter of time before Nipah—like HIV and Ebola before it—evolves the adaptations necessary to regularly jump from person to person. If it does, the next outbreak of Nipah may be more devastating than we can possibly imagine.

Organizations to Contact

The editors have compiled the following list of organizations concerned with the issues debated in this book. The descriptions are derived from materials provided by the organizations. All have publications or information available for interested readers. The list was compiled on the date of publication of the present volume; the information provided here may change. Be aware that many organizations take several weeks or longer to respond to inquiries, so allow as much time as possible.

American Society for the Prevention of Cruelty to Animals (ASPCA)
424 E. 92nd St.
New York, NY 10128-6804
phone: (212) 876-7700
email: publicinformation@aspca.org
website: www.aspca.org

Established as the first humane society in North America, the ASPCA believes that all animals are entitled to kind, respectful treatment by humans, and that laws should protect and guarantee these rights. The agency's mission is to prevent cruelty, help vulnerable animals, and keep pets safe in loving homes.

American Veterinary Medical Foundation (AVMF)
1931 North Meacham Rd., Suite 100
Schaumburg, IL 60173-4360
phone: (800) 248-2862
website: www.avma.org/Pages/home.aspx

The American Veterinary Medical Foundation advances animal health by being the leading US advocate for the veterinary profession. By supporting veterinary medical professionals, the agency promotes the health and welfare of animals.

Animal Health Institute (AHI)
1325 G St. NW, #700
Washington, DC 20005
phone: (202) 637-2440
website: www.ahi.org

The Animal Health Institute represents companies with an interest in veterinary health, and as a trade organization promotes the research, discovery, and development of animal medicines that keep animals and pets healthy.

Best Friends Animal Society
5001 Angel Canyon Rd.
Kanab, UT 84741-5000
phone: (435) 644-2001
email: info@bestfriends.org
website: www.bestfriends.org

This organization runs the largest no-kill shelter for companion animals in the US. Its mission is to bring kindness to animals, stop puppy mills, and bring about change so that no pets are homeless.

The Fund for Animals
200 W. 57th St.
New York, NY 10019
phone: (866) 482-3708
website: www.fundforanimals.org

The Fund for Animals has saved thousands of animals from suffering and cruelty. It provides sanctuary, veterinary, and rehabilitative services at three care centers in the United States.

The Humane Society of the United States (HSUS)
1255 23rd St. NW, Suite 450
Washington, DC 20037
phone: (202) 452-1100
email: donorcare@humanesociety.org
website: www.humanesociety.org

The Humane Society of the United States is an animal protection organization based in Washington, DC. This organization aims for a humane world both for people and animals, and because of this wants to end puppy mills, animal fighting, captive hunts, the wildlife trade, and factory farming.

Humane Society Wildlife Land Trust
1255 23rd St., NW, Suite 450
Washington, DC 20037
phone: (800) 729-SAVE
website: www.wildlifelandtrust.org

The Humane Society Wildlife Land Trust aims to protect the habitats of all wildlife. The agency preserves and manages permanent sanctuaries and natural habitats to achieve the goal of habitat preservation. It encourages private landowners to create habitat sanctuaries to preserve wildlife of all kinds.

PAWS
PO Box 1037
Lynwood, WA, 98046
phone: (425) 787-5711
website: www.paws.org

PAWS champions animal welfare through adoption, rehabilitation, education, and advocacy. The organization believes in the value of all animal life, and sees their mission as upholding the rights of companion animals, domesticated animals, and wild animals.

People for the Ethical Treatment of Animals (PETA)
501 Front St.
Norfolk, VA 23510
phone: (757) 622-PETA
website: www.peta.org

PETA is the largest animal rights organization in the world. It focuses its attention to help in the four areas where animals suffer: the entertainment industry, laboratories, the food industry, and the clothing industry. They protest the cruel killing of "pest" animals as well as domestic animals. They serve as a strong advocate for education through public service announcements advancing their idea that humans should not eat, wear, experiment on, use for entertainment, or abuse animals of any kind.

PetSmart Charities
19601 North 27th Ave.
Phoenix, AZ 85027
phone: (800) 423-PETS
email: info@petsmartcharities.org
website: www.petsmartcharities.org

The goal of PetSmart Charities is to find a lifelong loving home for every pet and prevent unwanted litters by sponsoring spay/neuter clinics. It finds homes for over 500,000 dogs and cats each year.

US Department of Agriculture (USDA)
1400 Independence Ave., SW
Washington, DC 20250
phone: (202) 720-2791
website: www.usda.gov

The USDA maintains an extensive online site covering twenty-nine agencies with jurisdiction over agriculture, natural resources, nutrition, food, and rural development in the United States. It is dedicated to innovation through best practices in science and management. The agency offers information on animal welfare, puppy mills, commercial animal breeding, and the Animal Welfare Act—the federal law that seeks to regulate the humane treatment of animals.

Bibliography

Books

Raymond Bial. *Rescuing Rover: Saving America's Dogs*. New York, NY: Houghton Mifflin, 2011.

Carol Bradley. *Saving Gracie: How One Dog Escaped the Shadowy World of American Puppy Mills*. Hoboken, NJ: Wiley Publishing, 2010.

Laura T. Coffey. *My Old Dog: Rescued Pets with Remarkable Second Acts*. Novato, CA: New World Library, 2015.

Rosaleen Duffy. *Nature Crime: How We're Getting Conservation Wrong*. New Haven, CT: Yale University Press, 2010.

Shelly Field. *Career Opportunities Working with Animals*. New York, NY: Ferguson's, 2012.

Liz Gogerly. *Caring for Animals*. Portsmouth, NH: Heinemann Library, 2012.

Kim Kavin. *The Dog Merchants: Inside the Big Business of Breeders, Pet Stores, and Rescuers*. New York, NY: Pegasus Books, 2016.

Ellie Laks. *My Gentle Barn: Creating a Sanctuary Where Animals Heal and Children Learn to Hope*. New York, NY: Harmony Books, 2014.

Peter Laufer. *Forbidden Creatures: Inside the World of Animal Smuggling and Exotic Pets*. Guilford, CT: Lyons Press, 2010.

Judy A. Mills. *Blood of the Tiger: A Story of Conspiracy, Greed, and the Battle to Save a Magnificent Species*. Boston, MA: Beacon Press, 2015.

Adrian R. Morrison. *An Odyssey with Animals: A Veterinarian's Reflections on the Animal Rights and Welfare*. New York, NY: Oxford University Press, 2009.

Laurel Abrams Neme. *Animal Investigators: How the World's First Wildlife Forensics Lab is Solving Crimes and Saving Endangered Animals.* New York, NY: Scribner, 2009.

Wayne Pacelle. *The Humane Economy: How Innovators and Enlightened Consumers Are Transforming the Lives of Animals.* New York, NY: William Morrow, 2016.

Jessica Pierce. *Run, Spot, Run: The Ethics of Keeping Pets.* Chicago, IL: The University of Chicago Press, 2016.

Amy Sutherland. *Rescuing Penny Jane: One Shelter Volunteer, Countless Dogs, and the Quest to Find Them All Homes.* New York, NY: HarperCollins, 2017.

Craig Welch. *Shell Games: Rogues, Smugglers, and the Hunt for Nature's Bounty.* New York, NY: William Morrow, 2010.

Peter Zheutlin. *Rescued: What Second-Chance Dogs Teach Us About Living with Purpose, Loving with Abandon, and Finding Joy in the Little Things.* New York, NY: TarcherPerigree, 2017.

Periodicals and Internet Sources

Rhett Butler, "Illegal Wildlife Trade in Asia Decimating Species, Warn Scientists," *Mongabay*, July 14, 2016. http://news.mongabay.com/2016/07/illegal-wildlife-trade-in-asia-decimating-species-warn-scientists/.

Tricia Conahan, "Ron Danta: "There's A Real World Out There," *Practical Horseman*, March 5, 2018. http://practicalhorsemanmag.com/personalities/ron-danta-theres-a-real-world-out-there.

Tucker J. Coombe, "A Dog's Life," *Cincinnati Magazine*, October, 2005. http://www.tuckercoombe.com/wp-content/uploads/2016/06/shelteredpawspdf.pdf.

Sean Gallagher, "Exotic Pet Owners of Beijing—In Pictures," *The Guardian*, September 20, 2017. http://www.theguardian. com/environment/gallery/2017/sep/20/exotic-pet-owners-beijing-china-endangered-in-pictures.

Mirren Gidda, "The Latest Illegal Business in the UK Is Dog Smuggling," *Newsweek*, January 16, 2018. http://www. newsweek.com/2018/01/26/illegal-business-uk-dog-smuggling-781508.html.

Sarah Hansen, "Adoption from Shelter vs. Buying from a Breeder: What's Best for You?" *Labrador Training HQ*, January 15, 2018. http://www.labradortraininghq.com/ labrador-puppies/adoption-vs-breeder-whats-best/.

Marjorie Ingall, "Why Rescuing Animals Is a Family Affair for This Maine Couple," *Real Simple*, March 29, 2017. http:// www.realsimple.com/work-life/family/pets/animal-rescue.

Aidan Jones, "Why Exotic Animal Trade Grows in Asia," *Christian Science Monitor*, January 28, 2012. http:// www.csmonitor.com/World/Asia-Pacific/2012/0128/Why-exotic-animal-trade-grows-in-Asia.

Rebecca Liebson, "Prison Dog Training Programs Rehabilitate Canines and Cons," *Clear the Shelters*, August 8, 2017. http://www.cleartheshelters.com/Prison-Pup-Programs-Give-Inmates-and-Shelter-Dogs-a-Second-Chance-437660633.html.

Katarzyna Nowak, "The World Has a Chance to Make the Wild Animal Trade More Humane," *National Geographic*, February 26, 2016. http://news.nationalgeographic. com/2016/02/160226-animal-trade-animal-welfare-exotic-pets-cites-wildlife-trafficking/.

Rachel Nuwer, "Asia's Illegal Wildlife Trade Makes Tigers a Farm-to-Table Meal," *New York Times*, June 5, 2017. http:// www.nytimes.com/2017/06/05/science/animal-farms-southeast-asia-endangered-animals.html.

Paul Solotaroff, "The Dog Factory: Inside the Sickening World of Puppy Mills," *Rolling Stone*, January 3, 2017. http://www.rollingstone.com/culture/features/the-dog-factory-inside-the-sickening-world-of-puppy-mills-w457673.

Scott Stump, "How These Prison Dogs and Inmates Are Changing Veterans' Lives," *Today*, March 24, 2017. http://www.today.com/series/veterans/prison-inmates-train-service-dogs-help-military-veterans-t109562.

Index